They Called Him Rabbi

MERVYN A. WARREN

Nampa, Idaho | Oshawa, Ontario, Canada
www.pacificpress.com

Copyright © 2017 by Pacific Press® Publishing Association
Printed in the United States of America
All rights reserved

The author assumes full responsibility for the accuracy of all facts and quotations as cited in this book.

You can obtain additional copies of this book by calling toll-free 1-800-765-6955 or by visiting http://www.adventistbookcenter.com.

Scripture quotations marked NIV® are taken from the THE HOLY BIBLE, NEW INTERNATIONAL VERSION®. Copyright ©1973, 1978, 1984, 2011 by Biblica, Inc.® Used by permission. All rights reserved worldwide.

Library of Congress Cataloging-in-Publication Data

Names: Warren, Mervyn A., author.
Title: They called him rabbi : a biography of Calvin E. Mosley, Jr. / Mervyn A. Warren, Ph.D., D. Min.
Description: Nampa : Pacific Press Publishing Association, 2017. | Includes index.
Identifiers: LCCN 2017013001 | ISBN 9780816362943 (pbk.)
Subjects: LCSH: Mosley, Calvin E., 1906-2001. | Seventh-Day Adventists—Biography.
Classification: LCC BX6193.M685 W37 2017 | DDC 286.7092 [B] —dc23 LC record available at https://lccn.loc.gov/2017013001

March 2017

Table of Contents

Foreword and Introduction 5

Acknowledgments and Dedication 8

CHAPTERS

    R i s i n g 9

    A d v a n c i n g 17

    B e c o m i n g 27

    B e s p e a k i n g 49

    I n t e r m i t t i n g 95

Chronology of Life and Service of Calvin E. Moseley, Jr. 101

Lighthearted Looks Along the Landscape 107

Pastors of Oakwood University Church 116

Sources 117

Index 119

About the Author 123

Foreword and Introduction

"C'mon, let's talk with my dad. It's time we share with him what we've been thinking about lately." "Okay, I fully agree." My agreement, however, bore some nervousness because of the nature of our recent thoughts. Being Oakwood College students, my special friend Barbara and I were well aware that her visiting father and Board of Trustees member, Elder Calvin E. Moseley, would be listening for a progress report of her college studies. Out of courtesy, he might inquire about mine. But the conversations she and I were having of late focused on another matter, something other than just finishing college and going to grad school. We were massaging the notion of getting married before graduation. Marriage? How would her father respond to his sophomore daughter and her senior boyfriend dreaming of pre-graduation matrimony? Why the rush? What's going on? Had we sought counsel from our campus pastor and teachers?

Less than a decade before this particular campus visit, Elder Moseley had resigned the chairmanship of the Religion Department of Oakwood and accepted the invitation to serve in the General Conference of Seventh-day Adventists as Assistant Director of the Regional Department headquartered in Takoma Park, Maryland—a suburb of Washington, DC. On campus for the Board of Trustees session, he hardly expected an agenda from us which, at least potentially for him, might distract from institutional business. Understandably, he always looked forward to returning to the Oakwood campus from time to time where, prior to his tenure with the GC, he had served so valiantly (1934-51) as the first African American chairman of Religion and pastor of the Oakwood College Church. More importantly on this trip, he wanted to spend time with his younger daughter, Barbara, who had been living on this selfsame campus from birth through this her present sophomore year.

At any rate, the moment of truth arrived when Barbara, her father, and I sat down together and moved briefly but not abruptly beyond conversational pleasantries to the real thing on my heart and hers. Approaching the nervous moment of truth, I did a mental dress rehearsal trying to predict the way the conversation might go—what I would say, how he might respond. On the one hand, I thought about something akin to Armageddon. On the other hand, a sense of inevitability came over me, settling my heart rate to expect nothing worse than "no." Taking a deep breath, I asked for permission to wed his daughter in the near future, like right after her present sophomore year which was my senior year.

With tact born of divine wisdom, Elder Moseley never used the word "no" but rather expressed his wish that we think instead about *after* Barb's completion of her baccalaureate degree. Without skipping a beat, he promised the green light would then be awaiting us with his full backing and support. He kept his promise when about two years later on June 15, 1959, Barbara Moseley became Barbara Warren—she a graduate of Columbia Union College (aka Washington Adventist University) and I a ministerial student at the Seventh-day Adventist Seminary of Potomac University (aka Andrews University).

From that day to this, I have been a son-in-law in awe of his father-in-law whose life and legacy I tread softly in attempting a written narrative. Frankly, if someone else had already done a formal Moseley biography, I would be perfectly satisfied. I did find very helpful material in the Oakwood University archives, especially an unpublished paper on his life and ministry by Elder Walter W. Starks, a former student of Elder Moseley and subsequent pastor and conference administrator on several levels in the SDA church. From the best I can determine, the Starks manuscript reads more like written notes of an extended conversation whose typed account was completed in 1988, about seventeen years into the Moseley retirement of

1971. Although not formally documented by sources and, therefore, considered anecdotal, his material is engagingly personal. Furthermore, his ninety page script complies generally with all I know and have researched so far. In my opinion, his informal material deserves special acknowledgment and, therefore, is warmly referenced in this narrative.

Elder Calvin Edwin Moseley, Jr. Students call him "Rabbi." Others say "Mose." His wife's favorite was "Hun" while his daughters' is "Daddy." I knew him as "Elder." His eulogists crowned him "The Father of Preachers" for having taught and prepared in his day at least up to ninety percent (90%) or more of African American pastors and evangelists for SDA pulpits. If you ever knew the man, whatever your choice or preferred sobriquet might have been, you surely became conscious of connecting with a life rich in honor, homiletics, humanitarianism, heroism, humor, horticulture, honeybees, hospitality, harmony, hymnody, and heaven. You also knew he was all about holding aloft the gospel banner of Jesus Christ and being a "voice crying in the wilderness" preparing "the way of the Lord" and making "His paths straight." (Matthew 3:3)

Mervyn A. Warren, Ph.D., D.Min.

Acknowledgments

You quickly learn on the safari of putting pen to paper that no one travels alone. Principal supporters in this project have been: Paulette Johnson, Librarian, Eva B. Dykes Library of Oakwood University; Clara (Peterson) Rock, first Archivist of Oakwood University (1972-85) whose landmark interviews and collections of Oakwood legends will always be foundational; Heather Rodriquez-James, former Archivist of Eva B. Dykes Library of Oakwood University; Odalys Miranda Suastegui, present Archivist, Eva B. Dykes Library of Oakwood University; Kanique Mighty-Nugent, Integrated Marketing and Public Relations of Oakwood University; Benjamin Baker, General Conference Archives; James H. Melancon, photographer, former acting Religion Department chair and faculty retiree; Roland Scott, photographer; and several unnamed former students and fellow-servants of Calvin Edwin Moseley, Jr. who, when hearing about my intended journey here, shared with me their touch of knowing, appreciating, and loving the man they knew as "Rabbi."

Dedication

To all who appreciate or practice the preaching and Bible tradition of the School of Religion at Oakwood University for which Calvin Edwin Moseley, Jr. laid the first building blocks.

RISING
a
b
b
i

    Demopolis? First hearing the name, you may think it sounds so un-Alabamian. In fact, for me initially, it was a throw-back to "Acropolis" in the Bible book of Acts chapter 22 where Paul delivers his famous speech on a high elevation of Mars Hill in Athens, Greece. Somehow, I suspected the words "Demopolis" and "Acropolis" had a kindred history. True enough, both are of Greek origin and wear the identical suffix ("polis" meaning "city"), thus Demopolis so named for "city of the people" while Acropolis being the "high city" focal point of the famed Mars Hill in Athens. It was not too much of a stretch for me to derive from their etymology a prediction of sorts that a son would be born in a city of the people in Alabama and rise to a destiny of rare service for God in high places. By the turn of the twentieth century, the Demopolis census reported a 2,606 population which rose to 7,377 by 1960, then continuing to at least 7,000 into the twenty first century through 2014, the largest city in Marengo Country.

    There Calvin Edwin Moseley, Jr., was born on January 6, 1906 to Lillie Belle (Dixon) Moseley who was a mid-wife and to Calvin Edwin Moseley, Sr. who worked at the plastering trade. Slightly over 2,500 in population at the time, Demopolis situated itself at the confluence of the Tombigbee and Black Warrior Rivers in north Marengo County just below the equator of the state toward southern Alabama. Founded between 1817 and 1821, after the fall of Napoleon's Empire and named by French expatriates and other French migrants who settled in the United States, the city's name was chosen to honor the democratic ideals behind the people-centered endeavor.

Early history of the area reveals an ethnic "coat of many colors" embodying native Americans, African Americans, French, German, Spanish, Swedish, English, and Irish. While Calvin, Sr., was of obvious African descent, Lillie Belle his wife bore clear clues also of European lineage with forebears from England, Germany, and Ireland. Her father happened to be German Jew whose tombstone inscription found by Calvin's younger brother Earnest reads, "James Hughes Dixon, born in Berlin, Germany." Mr. Dixon managed to father two families, one white and one black who functioned as separate groups but fully aware of each branch. Calvin, Jr. and brother Ernest and their immediate offspring remember that grandfather Dixon was known to them as "Santa Claus." Lillie Belle was one of seven children born to her mother and father. This maternal side of the family (father James Hughes Dixon and three of his sons) were painters and paper hangers. Two brothers of father James operated the largest grocery business in Demopolis. A sister of Lillie Belle "inherited" a drug store and two food stores at the death of her husband which were then managed by her six sons. On the paternal side of the family, father Calvin, Sr. had an aunt who became a school principal while another close relative owned and operated a barber shop—all in Demopolis, city of the people. In other words, examples of industry, diligence, and work among relatives provided role models and motivational backdrop for brothers Calvin, Jr. and Ernest to aspire and rise above the ordinary.

This is not to overlook racial tensions and social sensitivities of the Demopolis environment. On occasions, Calvin, Sr. and mother Lillie Belle as husband and wife found it the better part of wisdom that she take a seat in the back of their jalopy due to her very light skin complexion while her husband sat up front at the steering wheel posing as a chauffeur "driving Miss Daisy." Apparently, however, the atmosphere seemed sufficiently peaceful and livable that descendants would value perpetuating their heritage. Decades later, Calvin Edwin, Jr. and wife Harriet would attend "The Weiss-Sledge Family Reunions" a biennial gathering (which to this day into the twenty-first century) continues their family camaraderie and remembrances. But let us not get ahead of the Calvin E. Moseley, Jr. story.

Calvin, Jr. had not only a younger brother named Ernest but also a sister who died in infancy. Although Calvin and Ernest enjoyed a rather normal, carefree, fun-filled, energetic boyhood, their parents taught them very early the value and virtues of honest labor. Nevertheless, to them and their young peers, four seasons comprised their year: seasons of "marbles," "tops," "kites," and "baseball." Yet, in the Moseley household, making a living was very serious business. Having learned the plastering trade from a Seventh-day Adventist church brother named Ed Jones, the father of Calvin, Jr. and Ernest passed on to them the ability to plaster while also encouraging them to stay in school and complete their academic education. Father Calvin spurred them along this two dimensional track despite his being a "teenage dropout" or maybe because of it.

That two track pattern of school and work had been set for Calvin, Sr. himself before his two sons were born. When in high school, he met his future wife, Lillie Belle Dixon.

Their budding romance burst into full bloom, and both considered themselves sufficiently mature to marry which they did—he only nineteen and she a "sweet sixteen." Now for sure, Calvin, Sr. would need to throw his plastering skill and growth of income into full gear, face the responsibilities of manhood and maturity, and support the joy of marrying his "school girl sweetheart." Passing through the threshold of marriage, however, its thrills and merriments notwithstanding, Calvin, Sr. faced the reality of dwindling work opportunities in Demopolis brought on by slowdown of the construction market. Like all serious plasterers, he would move from place to place—wife and sons in tow—to wherever his trade would bring gainful employment. Though not a religious man at the time in the sense of having a formal creed, one thing for sure, his family came first, a standard whose principle (though probably unknown to him) clearly reflected the Biblical precept of Paul the apostle who says in 1 Timothy 5:8, "If anyone does not provide for his . . . immediate family, he . . . is worse than an unbeliever." (NIV)

Continuous search for employment led the Moseley family across the Alabama state line to Meridian, Mississippi, fifty-six miles west where abundant work rose to a respectable level. Here Calvin, Sr. set up residence and headquarters for his life and labor. The Meridian move also launched his sons' formal education in a private parochial school. Calvin, Jr. later said the private educational program developed for him a deeper interest in religious matters which he found continual delight in rehearsing to his parents the Bible stories learned.

That interest for Calvin, Jr. grew and with it a vivid imagination triggered by a film he viewed of the crucifixion of Jesus Christ. How impressed was he of the dramatic scene? The six year old persuaded his younger brother Ernest of three to allow his hands and feet to be tied to a wooden cross which he and playmates had made. The group raised and leaned the cross and its victim against the wall of the house. Was it not time now for an audience?

So thrilled with their achievement, the one playing like a motion picture producer, Calvin, Jr., hastened to call his mother to behold the wonderful production. In astonishment and alarm she rushed to the rescue. The playmates of Calvin, Jr. took their flight at her forceful reprimand. Although his imagination had promise, he learned he could not always portray Biblical scenes too literally.

Whether in Demopolis or Meridian, his pace and level of learning particularly during pre-teen years placed him in classes where he was the youngest pupil and told by classmates he was too young to compete. He met the challenge with determination and scholarship excelling in spelling, math, and geography. Another unique situation forced him to just roll with the punches. His teacher and principal at the Demopolis school (before moving to Meridian) happened to be his "Aunt Minnie." She sought to shield him from potential harassment by other students because of his scholarship at such a young and tender age. Her solution? Sweet old auntie showed her impartiality as principal-teacher by giving her nephew Calvin, Jr. lower marks and grades than he deserved. How injustice aided justice in this case, we may find it difficult to explain. Perhaps in context of "family," considering all dynamics unknown to us today, conceivably the teacher saved little nephew from potential irreparable damage inflicted by older bullies. Well, that's my apologia. What are your thoughts? Nicknamed "Dumpty" or sometimes "Dump" due to his being stocky, maybe a bit ovoid, and well-built, Calvin, Jr. could conceivably discourage some student bullies, but Aunt Minnie was not taking any chances. Nothing distracted her watch-care over her nephew.

Reaching his early teens, Calvin's feelings of romance began to surface. At that same time, the United States was engaged in World War I, and the spirit of patriotism soared high. Students in his class were assigned by Aunt Minnie to write a paper on war bonds whose purchase greatly helped to finance the war. Calvin put his pen to work but not on war bonds. Instead, to a female classmate he wrote: "My dear loving pretty one, as sure as the grass grows round the stump, you are my darling sugar lump." Beginning to warm up to his subject with even more elaborate expression, all of a sudden he lost his romantic musing replaced by a heavy strap dancing heavily across his back by none other than his "favorite" aunt. Needless to say, classmates went delirious with laughter, and Calvin, Jr. flushed with shame. It became very clear to him that romance in the classroom was not the time or place. He sobered up, learned well his lesson, and went on to win first place in his essay on "Baby Bonds and Thrift Stamps." His achievement, published on the front page of the Demopolis Daily newspaper, marked another milestone toward his rise to personal development and maturity. Learning priorities owed eternal thanks to an ever watchful Aunt Minnie.

Reaching the age of twelve or so, he could clearly say that among flying kites, shooting marbles, spinning tops, and playing baseball, the latter became his favorite and in due time his downfall. When he played the game confidently and daringly tossing his protective catcher's mask aside while positioned behind the batter, one day the ball ricocheted from a foul ball tip, landed on his unprotected forehead just above his eyes, causing him to "lick the dust." Calvin's customary decisiveness turned him away from playing baseball and flipped his attention to other interests—one of which was music for example.

He said later on in life that one of his earliest brushes with music that really entered his conscious awareness came from a black man named Kit who was both blind and a store owner. Kit would often walk through the neighborhood singing while peddling his wares. A number of his songs were Negro spirituals sung lustily and leaving their imprint on an impressionable young mind. Calvin, Jr. often lay in bed, listening to this singing as people would come out to hear the sightless singer and coax him along by shouting: "Sing it, Kit, sing it!" And sing it he did, rhythmically counting his steps, beating time with his cane while hawking his commodities throughout the community. His tunes reached into the heart of a pre-adolescent youngster who, when not outside to witness Kit, listened through the walls of his room. Who would have guessed that the same boy decades into the future would himself show special talent, perhaps even genius, for melody and harmony, lyrics and rhythm? Who would have foreseen his musical aptitude expressed later in the halls of higher education as well as church environs all over America?

The spiritual journey of Calvin, Jr. actually began quite early when at his mother's knee he heard her portraying in song the misery of helpless and unfortunate infants and parents. One line of a song that brought tears to his young eyes and stuck with him over the years are: "Gnats and flies picking in their eyes, poor little baby needs mommie." The vivid picture of such a pitiful plight formed a background which fanned the flames of his inner desire to become a Christian. Most people in the little town of Demopolis were religious and professed to being Baptists or Methodists. Calvin was sent to Baptist Sunday School and remembered that from time to time revivals lasting one or two weeks were conducted by either the pastor or guest preachers. Front pew was reserved for what they called the "mourners' bench" where sinners and mourners would sit and show their desire to "get religion." Eventually, Calvin, Jr. as an adolescent made his way to the "mourners' bench" to "get religion and come through." Three consecutive years without success, however, meant for him that if not now maybe later he would realize a sincere relation with God for which he longed. Meanwhile, he placed religion on the "back burner." Yet his mind would frequently recall the setting and faith of those who testified to have "come through" and who sang a little song that declared: "I died one time, ain't gonna die no more." "The Lord took my feet out of the miry clay and put them on a rock to stay." For Calvin, Jr. himself, fires of conversion were temporarily banked to burst into flame at a future time of God's own choosing. In the meantime, he would continue rising and developing toward promise and fulfillment.

Rabbi Advancing

"What are little boys made of?" inquires the nursery rhyme and then answers, "Snips and snails and puppy dogs tails. That's what little boys are made of." To that you might add playgrounds and swimming pools and ball games and hide-and-seek and just hanging out with playmates, and you might expect to cover the boyhood of Calvin, Jr. and younger brother Ernest. Instead, however, such typical after school activities were dispelled to a large degree by father Calvin, Sr, who placed into his sons' young hands the "hawk and the trowel" for plastering. Calvin, Jr. proudly recalled later that beginning as a twelve year old he worked on his independent plastering job and earned a handsome salary of $10.50 a week, as much as some adults. When asked by his father, "What are you going to do with the money," Calvin, Jr. responded, "I'm going to save it and put it in the bank." A pleased and permissibly proud father replied, "That's good, for you must have something to attend college." Unlike Calvin, Sr. who dropped out of school, Calvin, Jr. was not to look upon the plastering trade necessarily as his professional goal although the work was honest and honorable. The attractive salary plastering notwithstanding, professional options never hurt. Therefore, seeds were planted in the minds of the Moseley brothers to think of advancing to whatever and wherever formal education would provide.

Remember the close overseeing by Aunt Minnie that withheld acknowledging the academic excellence of nephew Calvin, Jr. for the sake of sheltering him from possible taunting or something worse by older students who resented his being "skipped" into their higher class? Remember her wish to steer away from any charge of favoritism or nepotism on her part? Well, his senior class teacher, Professor Jones, harbored no such inhibitions. He let the chips fall where they may, and upon examining the records found Calvin, Jr. to qualify for valedictorian of his class. Graduation had to be held in the Demopolis city theater to compensate for the lack of space to accommodate the audience in the school auditorium. Seating capacity of the theater? Approximately 1,500. Graduation attendance? The place was practically full. It was the night of nights, the event of events. Excitement and anticipation filled the air.

Leading up to graduation, on the one hand, the idea of competition for excellence among students is normally accepted by one's peers. On the other hand, competition by a much younger student whose achievements excel that of his older schoolmates is seldom welcomed with outstretched arms and loud applause. Similar dynamics tinted the situation of Calvin, Jr. Nevertheless, rather than being crushed or despondent, he applied himself to greater effort determining not to rank lower than any other student in his class and studying with increased zeal and dedication. Facing his ultimate reward of valedictorian and what the honor meant for him on graduation day, he had already begun possessing some degree of awareness of his musical ability but no evidence whatsoever of any talent for public speaking. He would soon come to know of a new found potential in oral communication which divine enabling was birthing for use in future years. At the graduation moment, however, human eyes could not yet see this fledgling fifteen year old unknowingly dress rehearsing for a proleptic assignment toward the classroom and pulpit on the world stage for Jesus Christ.

How did the valedictorian speech in 1921 turn out? First of all, the speech was prepared by Principal Jones who happened to be also Calvin's teacher. As Calvin recounts the graduation events decades later on, he recalls being caught up in the excitement of the moment. Looking into what seemed to him an endless sea of faces, inspiration seized him and fright vanished. The oration flowed with natural exhilaration and swept him to his grand climax, concluding with the words: "Alabama! Alabama! Alabama! We will always be true to thee!" Warm, enthusiastic, spontaneous audience response rang throughout the auditorium: "Do it again! Do it again!" Money coins rained appreciatively upon the stage. The gathered assembly stood to its feet as one person, and Calvin gave a repeat performance. Indeed, a young star was rising in Demopolis and destined to advance to plateaus known only by God.

Tuskegee Institute

Flashes from that star would lead to Tuskegee Institute where Calvin, Jr. at fifteen enrolled on the high school level hoping eventually for civil engineering (encouraged by his father), but electrical engineering was the closest vocation offered there. Calvin, Jr. himself thought he would finish at Tuskegee and, at the urging by some of his relatives, then head for Howard University to study law. That which influenced him most lastingly at Tuskegee came not from academic programs per se but rather from a person, namely, Dr. George Washington Carver already famous for his exploits in agricultural science. Having attainted a bachelor's degree in 1894 and a master's degree in 1896 from Iowa State College of Agriculture (now Iowa State University) and begun his teaching and research career at Tuskegee the same year (1896), Dr. Carver had already completed about twenty-five years of peerless service by the time Calvin arrived there in 1921. As a matter of fact, Carver joined the Tuskegee faculty in 1896 at the invitation of Principal Booker T. Washington. But when the teenager from Demopolis met Dr. Carver, he came to know *much more* than a scientist and one whom history would label the "Father of Modern Agriculture."

That Carver was a man of science is true. That he revolutionized agricultural science with his crop-rotation method and cultivation of soil-enriching crops such as peanuts and soybeans is also true. That he discovered over 100 uses for the sweet potato and 300 for the peanut is true. That his scores of derivatives from the peanut comprise such products as cooking oil, axle grease, printer's ink, beverages, dyes, cosmetics, paints, medicines, food products and scores more is true. That he chose not to patent his discoveries because, in his own words, "if I did it would take so much time [and] I would get nothing else done . . . [nevertheless] I don't want my discoveries to benefit specific favored persons" is true. That Carver was a deeply devoted Christian and attributed inspiration of his work to God and said, "Never since have I been without this consciousness of the Creator speaking to me . . . The out of doors has been to me more and more a great cathedral in which God could be continuously spoken to and heard from" is true. That Calvin E. Moseley, Jr. found (beyond the scientific genius of Carver) the spiritual side of the man equally compelling and a "man of God" as well as a "man of science" is also true.

It all started when Calvin was invited by Dr. Carver to visit his Bible study sessions. Personal contact with Dr. Carver was taking place periodically when the young student from Demopolis worked as "messenger boy" and delivered messages around campus from the office of President Robert Moton, successor to Dr. Booker T. Washington who passed in 1915. A relative of Calvin's father encouraged his parents to send the fifteen year old Calvin, Jr. to Tuskegee. That Calvin might be under his relative's supervision, he was assigned a job in the president's office where his relative was also working. His job meant also getting mucilage from Dr. Carver's office, stamp and seal letters, and take them to the post office. This constant contact led to a personal interest in Calvin which grew into a closeness which Dr. Carver felt so comfortable with that he allowed Calvin to call him by his first name, if he so chose. For certain, Dr. Carver saw an opening opportunity to witness for Christ, which led to his inviting Calvin to the Carver Bible study sessions.

Calvin became a regular attendant to the Bible studies, liked what he heard, and often remarked decades later how clearly he remembered being so deeply impressed by Dr. Carvers' scriptural teachings. Among the various Bible lessons, the Old Testament book of Deuteronomy with its declaration of "blessings and curses" (chapters 27 through 30) clung for a lifetime to Calvin's memory. The Biblical narrative portrays Moses with his elders delivering to the Israelites their marching orders preparatory to advancing into the promised Canaan. Time and time again, forty or so years after the Tuskegee experience when "Calvin" had become "Elder Moseley," I would hear his reflecting and reminiscing about those vivid "blessings and curses." You might say the intersection of Calvin's life with that of Dr. Carver's on the Tuskegee campus proved crucial in a religious way of enhancing and advancing Calvin's appreciation for Bible and things spiritual. For sure, a look at the life of George Washington Carver ushers you into a special sanctuary where you see God and science walking hand in hand in loving friendship. One of the stories passing down the corridors of time finds Carver and God having a conversation. One version of their exchange goes like this:

Carver: "Lord, please teach me all about your universe."
God: "That's quite a tall order, George. Ask for something more in proportion to your little mind."
Carver: "How about teaching me about the earth?"
God: "That mind of yours still wants to know far too much."
Carver: "Well, Lord, why did you make human beings?"
God: "I'm afraid, George, that also is beyond your comprehension."
Carver: "Would you tell me all about plants?"

God:	"Sorry, my son, too large an order for you."
Carver:	"Then, Lord, I meekly ask you to just tell me about the peanut."
God:	"Now, that's more your size. I'll grant you the mysteries of the peanut."

History records the extended response of God to Carver as saying: "I will grant you the mystery of the peanut. Take it inside your laboratory and separate it into water, fats, oils, gums, resins, sugars, starches, and amino acids. Then combine these under my three laws of compatibility, temperature and pressure. Then you will know why I made the peanut." Taking an extended moment here on Dr. Carver provides valuable backdrop for a lifelong love affair Calvin had with his dualistic understanding of the God of the Bible and the God of nature being one in the same.

A particular academic challenge, however, was coming to surface. Looking back on those Tuskegee days, the Demopolis reports that his language needed a bit of "moral tailoring." The coloring of language used for emphasis by rough men of the Demopolis community as well as also by some of Calvin's relatives had bled into his regular vocabulary and accompanied him to Tuskegee. Although his less than desirable language may not have been dominant, his formal grammar suffered ignominiously. To gain entrance into Tuskegee required an English examination which, when taken by Calvin, exposed his grammar and raised some eyebrows. His examiner did a "double take" when looking at his *grades* on the one hand and then at his *grammar* on the other hand because the former was belied by the latter and caused complete astonishment. "Are you sure this is your record?" asked the examiner. Calvin replied, "Yassuh." When needing to respond in the negative, Calvin would answer, "Norsuh." The examiner remarked, "Your grades are very good, but your language is abominable." Not in the vocabulary of the young Calvin, the word "abominable" caused him to wonder if his examiner had taken to swearing. However, having been taught the habit of consulting the dictionary by his "Aunt Minnie," he added the word "abominable" to his language repertoire and advanced his vocabulary bank by one.

Further help would be on the way to address the language problem. A cousin of Calvin's, James Flood, who happened also to be secretary to President Moton, offered a judicious and discreet hand. Though Calvin was only a junior, cousin James arranged for him to sit at the table with seniors and placed him in the tutelage hands of a young lady in whom his cousin had confidence. She was known for proficient English grammar and was told by James: "This boy is a relative of mine. His language is very poor. I want you to see if you can help him." And help him she did. During one tutoring session while sitting at the campus dining room table, she asked Calvin a question to which he replied, "I does." Looking at him with serio-comic amusement, struggling to hold back her overwhelming urge to laugh out loud, she gained her composure and said: "Calvin, I never does. He does and she does, I do or I do not." His academic record thereafter confirmed his quickness of aptitude, and he never made that blunder again.

Tuskegee afforded the opportunity for coming into contact with and getting to know persons in key positions on campus. Dr. G. Lake Imes contributed to the musical and character development of Calvin especially accepting him at the recommendation of his cousin, Mr. Flood, into a club for boys called "The Careful Builders Club." The organization emphasized the development of Christian character and opened every meeting with prayer. Some of the members of the club had begun organizing a quartet and, made aware of the singing ability of Calvin (a high tenor at the time), invited him to join the group.

Continued progress in music came under the instruction of Mrs. Genesee (Jennie) Lee, skilled in the art of musical "sight reading." An accomplished musician in her own right, she directed the famous Tuskegee choir and invited Calvin to be a choir member. He demurred after noticing her strict discipline applied to those who made mistakes—a sharp crack on your bare knuckles with her baton. He became quite skillful, however, in sight reading which he credits to Mrs. Lee. Such training would serve him greatly in the future when preparing quartet and male chorus performances representing Oakwood College throughout North America. It might be said that arguably those future Oakwood choral groups directed by Calvin E. Moseley, Jr. were as famous in their sphere as Tuskegee groups were in their sphere which, actually, boomerangs credits to his stay at Tuskegee.

Another group activity curiously permitted at Tuskegee, while divisive in the black community, was dancing. It was permitted, however, under a strictly enforced condition that dancing took place with members of the same gender and avoid over familiarity with the opposite sex. Such an arrangement today in the twenty-first century might prompt another question related to same sex violations. For Calvin, this activity was short-lived as he had already begun to hear the beat of another drummer communicating through a number of personal experiences. For example, during the night when he and his dorm roommate lay asleep, they were awakened by a severe electrical storm of cracking thunder and flashing lightning blinding their waking eyes. Calvin himself was struck on his thigh by the lightning thus causing him to leap out of bed. Lightning clapped its hands again and knocked his roommate out of bed. On the leg of Calvin, the thunderbolt left its calling card, a red mark a foot long and an inch wide. What a sobering experience! Needless to say, very little sleeping took place while awaiting daybreak and listening to the raging storm growling in the background. The fact of being struck by lightning, yet not killed, left a lasting impression on the mind of Calvin, motivating him to more sincere efforts to walk the "straight and narrow way." Early home influences, exposure to Bible study by Dr. George

Washington Carver, and this near tragic encounter with mother nature prompted him to do more sober pondering. Tuskegee days were coming to an end, and instinctively Calvin knew something beyond lay ahead (though specifics were unclear at the moment), and he must ready himself to advance into history. His talent with the cornet assigned him the privilege of blowing taps each evening for the Tuskegee Institute campus. In his heart, taps was signaling him to something beyond.

BECOMING a rabbi

While Calvin was studying at Tuskegee, 1921-22, his father and mother with their younger son, Ernest, in tow moved to Jackson, Mississippi after living alternately in Demopolis (Alabama) and Meridian (Mississippi). There they were invited to an evangelistic meeting in progress and conducted by Elder J. H. Laurence and assisted by Elder F. L. Peterson. Ernest attended these Bible-focused meetings and was baptized later by Elder Frederick S. Keitts who had replaced the first two evangelists and concluded the meetings. Young Ernest wasted no time witnessing for Christ and invited his father, Calvin, Sr., to attend the preaching and worship gatherings. Calvin, Sr. had never made a confession of Christianity. Nevertheless, he frequented these evangelistic meetings, experienced conversion, and likewise was baptized into the Seventh-day Adventist Church. The mother, Lillie Belle (Dixon) Moseley, became the third family member to commit to God through Jesus Christ in this new setting of Adventist believers.

Calvin, Jr. left Tuskegee in 1922 and joined his family and new home in Jackson, Mississippi, and found the same evangelistic services still in progress. Bible tracts from those meetings were being sent to him all along by his family which he read while still at Tuskegee. Now that Calvin had come home, brother Ernest persuaded him to check the meetings out. He agreed and went to witness the Bible-based preaching for himself. On his very first night, the very first sermon he heard was "The Second Coming of Christ." Never before had he experienced such power of the Holy Spirit working on his heart. Once again the desire burned within for becoming a Christian. Looking back on that pivotal moment in his life, he recalled: "When I was baptized by Elder Keitts of Jackson, Mississippi, dripping wet with water, I went into the pastor's study and dropped to my knees and prayed a prayer similar to that Solomon prayed in 1 Kings 3:7, 9: 'Lord, I'm just a lad. I've joined your church. Will you just teach me how to go in and out among your people, and give me wisdom to be the kind of a Christian you want me to be.' No sooner had I prayed that prayer that it appeared to me I heard an inner voice: 'You will preach for Me.' I responded, 'Lord, I don't know anything about preaching. There aren't any preachers in my family.' That experience actually was the inspiration for my choice [to go to college and major in Bible]."

But school (at least Oakwood) would wait a year due to what he called being "stubborn." Whether his stubbornness meant a time in the valley of decision about returning to Tuskegee to study law or civil engineering or whether to pursue his newfound conviction of ministry by attending Oakwood Junior College, he never said. At any rate, during the one year or so interval in Jackson, Mississippi, Calvin, Jr. continued his education by attending Jackson College where he became a close friend of the president's son, played the coronet and trumpet skillfully, and made good use of having been taught sight reading by Genesee Lee, Tuskegee choir director. Here at Jackson College he found adventure in the field of music and joined the band. Meanwhile, he had two posts to lean on there in Jackson for encouragement in his newfound faith and walk with the Lord Jesus Christ: his immediate family and his new church family. Witnessing to fellow students at JC became another source of personal growth.

Conversion and Call

Over time decades later, Calvin would look in his rearview mirror at six early experiences he considered significant crossroads for his young spiritual journey of becoming converted to Jesus Christ and convicted for a life's work. His *first* pivotal moment dates back to 1921 when he attends Tuskegee Institute at fifteen years of age and develops an insatiable appetite and appreciation for the Scriptures due to campus Bible studies conducted by Dr. George Washington Carver.

Returning home after one year at Tuskegee, he joins his father, mother, and brother in Jackson, Mississippi, accepts Jesus Christ as his personal Savior, and submits to the rite of baptism. While still in his water-soaked baptismal robe, he finds himself in the pastor's study praying for divine guidance. Instantly he hears an inner voice saying to him: "I want you to preach for me." "Lord, I don't know anything about preaching. There aren't any preachers in my family," he responds. Although conversion to God through Jesus Christ and the Holy Spirit forms the basis for his baptism, the "call to preach" idea accompanies that experience and becomes *another* pivotal moment in the youthful life of the sixteen/seventeen year old.

A *third* landmark sees Calvin standing on a scaffold about thirty feet above a concrete foundation. While the teenager is plastering a school auditorium wall, he is noticed showing unusual behavior by Alfred Jones, a fellow plasterer and friend of his father. Several other plasterers confirm the unnerving sight. There stood Calvin, Jr., almost tottering, on the scaffold and, as if in a trance, keeps staring unsteadily toward the corner wall. Jones shakes him, asking excitedly: "What's happening to you, fella? What's wrong with you? I've been watching you. You're acting like a fool. You will fall through the scaffolding and break your neck. You stepped into as many holes as you stepped over. Yet, strangely, you did not fall through. I didn't know what to think." Calvin clearly knows what he himself was thinking but is ashamed to admit to his co-plasterer that he was visualizing the second coming of Jesus Christ in power and glory. A teary-eyed Calvin cannot claim conscious awareness of what his co-worker described about stepping in and around holes on that thirty foot scaffold above ground, and he does not try to explain it. He can only see the goodness of God in that incident, savor the change taking place in his life, and thereafter pegging the moment as consolidating his conversion experience.

Landmark *four* appears when Calvin lands at Oakwood Junior College in 1925. The curriculum requires Bible of all students regardless of major. Although ministry lingers in his mind, by now at Oakwood also a profession in business tugs at him. His Bible teacher (W. L. H. Baker whom he describes as "Australian and a very godly man") would be a profound spiritual influence along the path of life and decision making. Often the professor told the class about his time serving as secretary for Ellen G. White as well as blended his Bible instruction with other personal experiences while often shedding tears before the class. Baker's human touch solemnized everyone and breathed a serious atmosphere where once again Calvin hears God's voice speaking to Him saying: "I want you to preach for Me."

Calvin's typically demurring response followed: "Lord, I am afraid to preach." Of course, God has heard this all before. However, divine love keeps returning like a friendly echo. In retrospect, Calvin would look back at three influential factors by which Professor Baker helped to steady him, namely: his Bible class, one of his chapel addresses, and his homiletics/preaching class—primary influences bringing him back to reckon with a call to ministry. The question from God never changed. Calvin's response remains pretty much the same albeit with a different twist. His full response includes: "Lord, I feel I ought to preach. I have had the urge all these days, and yet I am afraid of it. Lord, I make You a promise. To make sure that You want me to preach, if You will arrange affairs in my life so that I will *become the pastor of a brand new church that is newly organized*. If you will do that for me, I will take that as proof

You really want me to preach." No sooner than offering this prayer and reconciling his thoughts to what He believes God would do, he surrenders and peace and calm set in. His decision gave him a platform on which to build his altar of commitment and be motivated for academic excellence by the statement read in his Christian education class by Mrs. Mary Tucker, wife of the Oakwood president (Joseph Tucker), a statement from the book of *Education* by Ellen White, page 18: *"Higher than the highest human thought can reach is God's ideal for His children. Godliness—godlikeness—is the goal to be reached. Before the student there is opened a path of continual progress. He has an object to achieve, a standard to attain, that includes everything good, pure, and noble. He will advance as fast and as far as possible in every branch of true knowledge. But his efforts will be directed to objects as much higher than mere selfish and temporal interests as the heavens are higher than the earth."* Like a rocket launched from its pad, the young Calvin is inspired and motivated to his highest potential. From that day forward at Oakwood, his grade-point-average rose higher and higher until during his last year and a half his average in all his classes equaled straight "A."

Now comes a *fifth* dose of confirmation dressed in a garb of personal illness right after his graduation from Oakwood Junior College in 1927. He had returned home in Jackson, Mississippi while trying to raise money, process in his heart the idea of ministry, and consider Emmanuel Missionary College (Michigan) to continue his education. This interval of time between graduating from Oakwood and time at home figuring out his next move finds him still having a tinge of wondering about ministry for life. Regretfully, returning home to continue celebrating graduation meets with a confining sickness. "I tried hard to evade the responsibility [ministry] until I was stricken for thirteen days with a near fatal illness—a severe case of typhoid fever," he would remember. Fortunately, his mother who was a former nurse is there to apply a popular treatment of that day, namely, hot baths to break the fever diagnosed as typhoid. About the fifteenth day, she places him again in a tub of more hot water, and suddenly Calvin faints. Everything turns to utter darkness. Out of his darkness, Calvin cries: "Mother, I can't see a thing! Please help me find the bed." Somehow she gets him out of the bathtub into the bed where he immediately begins thanking God. Just as immediately, he hears that voice all too familiar speaking to his heart: "Do you intend to preach for Me?" The freshly minted graduate replies: "Lord, You mean to tell me if I do not preach, I will not get out of this bed at all?" In solemn desperation comes his sincere vow to God: "Lord, I am making a promise. If You will get me out of this bed and keep me in good health, I will cooperate and do my best as You teach me to preach for You." The very next day his fever is broken, and by afternoon he's out of bed and on the front porch swing.

The Sabbath following Calvin's being healed of typhoid fever, his sickbed vow meets its test when the Moseley family decides to drive in their "little flivver Ford" to church in Vicksburg, Mississippi some forty or so miles away. Calvin himself has a special reason to look forward to hearing the minister preach. If declaring the gospel will be the pulpit task in his own future, then hearing someone else preach takes on a new dimension. He will now begin taking close notice on how preaching is done. He will now be not only a worshiper but also a "student" looking for sermon tips to provide help and instruction and fire his zeal as if in an observation class. But surprise of all surprises, as it turns out, the minister does not appear. Want to guess what happens next? The local church members instinctively looked to Calvin to stand in the breach, simply because he had recently graduated from Oakwood Junior College. He's the ram in the thicket simply because the general perception prevails that all students who attend Oakwood can automatically preach. Under this broad umbrella, they spontaneously waste no time in laying hands on Calvin, Jr. to bring "a word from the Lord" for His waiting people. Suddenly, Calvin remembers his day-old "sick bed vow" telling God that "If You get me out of this bed, I will do my best." In an unpredicted way, the future has suddenly become present. Time has now come for him to stand up and speak up! Under his conscious recollection of his vow, he rises to preach his very first sermon, and one whose content he could never recall years ahead. And understandably so, you must agree, given the pressure packed impromptu setting. He comes to church that Sabbath prepared to hear someone else deliver the message and, therefore, has no predetermined sermon text, sermon subject, or sermon content. Nevertheless, God so powerfully blesses his preaching that day until word got around and demanded more of his pulpit witness. Deeming the number six to be the sign of "man" in Scripture, this *sixth* crossroad in Calvin's conversion and conviction for a life's work consolidates his turning point from boyhood to manhood, youth to maturity.

Destination Oakwood Junior College

While spending much of 1923 and 1924 studying at Jackson College and working with his father (Calvin, Sr.) and brother (Ernest) as a plasterer, Calvin heard of but had not yet set foot on Oakwood soil. His first most direct contact with the Huntsville school happened when two Oakwood recruiters met him at his second camp meeting in Brookhaven, Mississippi. Ivan Christian (student) and Anna Knight (educator) appealed to him to enroll at Oakwood Junior College (J. I. Beardsley president). Calvin eventually consented to go to Oakwood. When he eventually arrived the next year, 1925, for summer school, Joseph A. Tucker had been appointed president. One of the first things on Calvin's agenda was to clear his head of thoughts of a business career sparked probably at Jackson College. Besides that ministry was gaining the inside track with him, nonetheless, there were intermittent tugs of war within as Calvin sifted through professional choices.

It is quite reasonable to assume that Calvin's arrival on campus brought with it a reputation of having studied at Tuskegee Institute and Jackson State College. Add to that his plastering trade and music ability (blowing the cornet/trumpet and singing), and you have a student with potential. Shortly after he registered at Oakwood, the regular campus quartet composed of Frank L. Peterson, John H. Wagner, Sr., Charles Salisberry, and Henry Hammond found itself facing a challenge. One of its members, Hammond, seemed averted to pinning himself down to "regular practice routine" which inevitably handicapped the group. Quartet practice with only a trio available became more and more difficult. Meanwhile, Peterson (faculty member and apparent leader of the quartet) had heard the voice of Calvin ringing out harmoniously during Friday evening vespers and subsequently invited him to try out for their quartet. Calvin's voice, once a tenor, after his leaving Jackson College grew heavier and heavier to a fully developed bass. He blended so well with the other singers that his tryout soon ripened into regular membership. Little did he know that his experience with this quartet would provide training and a forum for honing, improving, and embellishing his God-giving talent to its highest pinnacle for musical appreciation, composition, and performance in the context of Christian education and ministry.

Called the Oakwood Jubilee Quartet, they were the first extensive tour musical group for the school, mirroring in name and function the world famous Fisk Jubilee Singers of Fisk University who had been concertizing over fifty years since 1871. Recognizing the rich musical gifts of Oakwood students, President Tucker, though having been at Oakwood barely a year (1924) set out on a six weeks' nationwide recruitment tour accompanying his quartet troupe. It was about 1925 or so when Calvin joined the Oakwood Jubilee Quartet.

Starting with this singing group, future Oakwood generations expected that the school would always have a quartet to assist in student recruitment. Did up to six weeks away from classes pose a problem for these student singers? Certainly so. In retrospect decades into the future, Calvin expressed being in an uneasy predicament of missing classes. However, as he has said, teachers provided avenues for "study and report in outline form what we did while we were in journey. . . [and] somehow we were able to catch up and get along."

Instructional Influences

During his two years of studying at Oakwood Junior College, 1925-27, especially did three teachers stand out above others in his life. The first is Frank Loris Peterson whose fifteen or twenty minute worship sessions morning and evening in Butler Hall touched the student Calvin on a unique level which he had never experienced before. Being just a young Christian who knew very little about the Bible formally, he credits Elder Peterson with introducing him to so many things within and about the Bible which he had never heard or known before. His contact with Professor Peterson so inspired him that he fell in love with his Bible. Then there is Mrs. J. A. Tucker, wife of President Tucker, concerning whom Calvin remarked that if there ever were a godly woman, she certainly was. She taught him a course in education from the book by Ellen G. White bearing that title. One day in class, Calvin recited his memory gem which says: "Higher than the highest human thought can reach is God's ideal for His children. Godliness—Godlikeness—is the goal to be reached." Mrs. Tucker's lecture took off from there and challenged the students on going to the limit of their abilities for God. Calvin himself became electrified and never forgot that moment! As a matter of fact, when the teacher dismissed class, Calvin found a cedar tree along the way between the Old Chapel and Moran Hall, sat there mulling the memory gem over and over in his mind and was electrified all over again. He thought that "If that's what God wants me to do, I'm going to the top!" Sitting there and letting his imagination "run riot," he imagined reaching the pinnacle, the apex, as God's wish for him. On that his heart was fixed. Professor E. C. Jacobsen, teacher of World History, is the third person leaving a positive mark on Calvin who, while at Tuskegee Institute, hated history. Professor Jacobsen created in Calvin such a love for history until later at Emmanuel Missionary College he would choose history as a second major, and after EMC it would be history as a major briefly in graduate school, Northwestern University. But details of life after Oakwood will come later.

Let the Music Begin

The first extended tour by the Oakwood Jubilee Quartet began in Nashville, Tennessee at the Southern Publishing House chapel. Then they sang for the nearby Madison School and Sanitarium. From there the itinerary took them to St. Louis, Missouri and Clinton, Missouri and Clinton Theological Seminary, a German school presided over by Elder Dan Ochs (where Calvin first met him) who subsequently became Vice President for North America of the General Conference.

Other cities, places, and churches included Kansas City, Kansas and Missouri; Enterprise, Kansas; Wichita, Kansas; Pueblo, Colorado; Boulder, Colorado; Campion, Colorado; Denver, Colorado; Crawford, Nebraska; Shelton, Nebraska; College View, Nebraska; Nevada, Iowa (Oak Park Academy) and Cedar Rapids, Iowa (Iowa Sanitarium). *(Especially did Cedar Rapids hold warm memories in the heart of Calvin, because here was the home of his uncle—"my dad's only living brother, and I saw him for the first time in my mature years out there in Cedar Rapids.")* From there they traveled to Davenport, Iowa and on into Chicago, Illinois.

"We went to Chicago quite a number of times [subsequent to this first trip], and we had a great time there," Calvin has reminisced with a special lilt tingeing his voice. Yes, Chicago would indeed become a favorite place owing to his being introduced to a young lady there called "Miss Slater" by Mrs. T. Ann Jones, treasurer of the Shiloh SDA Church. He got to know her full name was Harriet Frances Slater, one active in church ministry particularly secretary of the Adventist Youth Society. Calvin himself has described her impressively as being "tall and rather pleasant to look at . . . . She had a long braid [and] it was plaited long enough for her to sit on. And as she moved off, I was attracted by that braid. That's the first time I ever saw her . . . . After that quartet trip, I kept her in memory." For sure, she became a person of prime interest for his future.

Meanwhile, this quartet (dressed in dark blue serge suits and bow ties) continued its inaugural tour. They delivered a repertoire of Negro spirituals, hymns, folk songs, work songs, and play songs from Chicago to the Hinsdale Sanitarium and up to Grand Rapids, Michigan; Cedar Lake, Michigan; Berrien Springs, Michigan (Emmanuel Missionary College/now Andrews University); Battle Creek, Michigan (Battle Creek College); Holly, Michigan; Jackson, Michigan. As Calvin has said, "Oh, we just went all over." At last, the quartet itinerary turned southward through Indianapolis, Indiana; Cicero, Indiana; Louisville, Kentucky (both churches there) and from Louisville "we were back on campus shortly." While the six-week tour did not fail Calvin in his classes, his absence did affect his scholarship causing him to receive the only "C" during his study at Oakwood.

It did not take him very long to realize his need to do a balancing act with his academics and his co-curricula music. Additional music opportunities inevitably poured in. Frank L. Peterson organized an octet of four females and four males for which Calvin sang bass. Among their appointments was also Graysville, Tennessee (antecedent to Southern Missionary College and Southern Adventist University). Names in the octet some of whom played important roles over time in developing and progressing the works for blacks in the south are Julia Baugh, Jennie Stratton, Viola Taylor, Alga Bailey, Frank L. Peterson, John H. Wagner, Charles Salisberry, and Calvin E. Moseley, Jr. Another group, the Male Chorus, had been directed by John H. Wagner with Calvin one of the singers, but Wagner's dropping out that year left a leadership void. The lot fell on Calvin to take over the Male Chorus and also the Band to boot. Like flowers after spring showers, opportunities for larger music experience continued coming his way thick and fast. Academia, nevertheless, found ways to keep pace. While the Jubilee Quartet was away on a singing trip, the senior class organized and elected a president. Because of some infraction, a reconsideration of the procedure led to a reversal of the presidential balloting; and the ensuing election elected Calvin senior class president.

Apparently, although the stage for Calvin's campus popularity held its own, his younger brother, Ernest, also an Oakwood student, was being discovered as a musician in his own right. The very year that Calvin completed his Oakwood studies, 1927, his younger brother sang in a couple of campus quartets one consisting of: S. B. Huddleston, Harvey Kibble, Charles Gray, and Ernest Moseley. Around the same time, he sang with another group including: Emile Jarreau, Otis Edwards, Harvey Kibble, and Ernest Moseley.

Regarding big brother Calvin, shortly after receiving that leadership honor mentioned above from fellow schoolmates and graduating from Oakwood Junior College in 1927, the college extended to him the privilege of attending the General Conference session of Seventh-day Adventists convening in Milwaukee, Wisconsin. A highlight of the gathering was the preaching of J. K. Humphrey, the former charismatic and controversial African American pastor of the Ephesus Church in Harlem, New York. For this General Conference assembly, the program called for Calvin to blow his trumpet. He chose to play "The Commodore Polka" which involved notes requiring triple tonguing expertise. The reception was so enthusiastically received that he had to do an encore of playing portions again. Further making this a pleasant occasion is the fact that it was not lost upon him that seated in the audience was the young lady from Chicago, Harriet Slater, whom he secretly admired.

Dreams of Emmanuel Missionary College

As the General Conference session drew to a close, President Joseph A. Tucker said to him, "Brother Moseley, why don't we spend the rest of the year student recruiting?" Calvin replied, "President Tucker, I plan to go to college next year if I can get some money. If you can help me get a scholarship to Emmanuel Missionary College instead of my plastering to get it, I'll sing with the quartet all summer long." The president had reservations about this being possible, and Calvin went home and back to his old trade of plastering. Meanwhile, panic set in. With employment at a minimum and the country inching toward a depression, Calvin became unable to enroll in school at all. For the greater part of one year (1927f.), he marked time dreaming about continuing his education and attaining the baccalaureate degree. This time spent out of school has been described by Calvin as the most disappointing and discouraging in his life. So much of a harvest time in informative study, exhilarating activities, and inspirational music at Oakwood now followed suddenly by a drought. It was a year of unemployment and inactivity. Over night, it seemed, his dream collapsed and his future faded. Was his time of great promise at Oakwood only a mirage in the desert?

Foresight had led his parents (Calvin, Sr. and Lillie Belle) to purchase nine acres of land outside of Jackson, Mississippi in the town of Bryan. The premises contained an old shanty which Calvin and his father reworked, building it into a modest home. This became their little "oasis" amid the national depression desert. Calvin further put his creative imagination to work in his room, giving it a facelift by plastering on the ceiling a design of bright clouds and blue skies forecasting hope for better days. But for now, instead, a cloud of another hue stalked at his door. Typhoid fever would be his bedfellow over two weeks followed by an opportunity to preach his very first sermon on the first Sabbath of his recovery referenced above. Not only did his impromptu message (due to an absentee speaker) lift the spirits of those who heard but also elate the spirit of him who preached and gave him deep confirmation of what he was to become and what his future would be about.

The next step in the mind of Calvin was to further his education. Advice from Addison Perkins, a member of his church in Jackson and himself a college graduate, rang steadily in his ears: "If you want to get a good education, in my opinion, the best school we have at this time is Emmanuel Missionary College." But Calvin's cash flow promised no position to follow up on his desire or Perkin's counsel. Despite the gloomy outlook, a beautiful thing happened that further demonstrated the character and commitment of the Moseley family to his education and preparation for service. While Calvin's own efforts at working hard all year to secure means to complete his education bore little or no financial fruit, and prospects for enrolling at EMC seemed exceedingly dark, his mother (knowing how anxious he was to complete his education) determined to do something to assist him.

She had no money, but the family had a homestead back in Demopolis, Alabama where he grew up. She drove to Demopolis from Jackson, sold the property to her father and Calvin's grandfather—James Hughes Dixon referred to earlier as originating from Berlin, Germany. When she returned from Demopolis, she placed two hundred and fifty dollars ($250.00) in the hands of Calvin and the same amount in the hands of his brother, Ernest and said: "Now boys, go to school." Ernest returned to Oakwood Junior College (now Oakwood University) in Huntsville, Alabama, and Calvin went to Emmanuel Missionary College in Berrien Springs, Michigan (now Andrews University).

Arriving at EMC in 1928 with only two hundred and fifty dollars ($250.00), Calvin lost no time seeking employment to augment his meager resources. How pleasant to meet his good friend J. K. Arms who was on the staff at Oakwood during Calvin's student days there. Mr. Arms knew Calvin to be a good plasterer and had observed his work at Oakwood in a number of areas—workshop, grounds, bricklaying, walkways, cement work and kindred areas of plastering and masonry. He witnessed Calvin's willingness to work and dedication to achieve and knew his attitude that "business came before pleasure." Such traits of character, learned and developed in early years, became his lifestyle and followed him through Oakwood. Mr. Arms, now Business Manager at EMC, not only greeted Calvin warmly but remembered his fidelity to duty. Providentially, his memory rewarded Calvin in a most handsome and profitable way. When the EMC chapel was built, the lower auditorium lay only partially complete. Although used for recreation, additional work needed to be done including plastering.

One day Mr. Arms said to him: "Brother Moseley, we are being pushed for more space, and we are going to have to develop this auditorium and big playground that we have into something more substantial. I talked to a plasterer in the community, but he is asking too much money, and the president will not agree to his price. How much would you charge to plaster the auditorium?" "How much is he asking?" responded Calvin and continued: "I will come under his price whatever it is." Mr. Arms replied: "He is asking twenty-five cents below the going wage." (At that time, it was three dollars and fifty cents per hour.) Calvin agreed to do it for half the price, and the deal was sealed.

An incident took place one night while Calvin was plastering that left an indelible imprint upon his mind. Up to that time, he had sustained only a passing acquaintance with President Guy F. Wolfkill, but a single night's experience brought about a change that would stand him in good stead for the remainder of his stay at EMC. While plastering the auditorium, a half hour before quitting time, his helper who mixed the mortar made a batch more than needed for the remaining work time. Facing Calvin was the predicament of letting the plaster sit over night and thereby be ruined or throw it away per the usual with surplus mortar or, option three, stay overtime until it's used all up. As you might imagine, plastering is no easy job, and when quitting time comes even the most faithful plasterer is fully exhausted. Even when paid overtime, he is not too anxious to continue working after hours. Despite the fact that the excess plaster on hand could not be charged to some mistake on the part of Calvin, he decided to forego his fatigue and continue working until all excess mortar was used up even though it cost his missing supper. He simply could not see the school losing money by conscious waste. He decided to remain on the job, miss supper, and finish the job.

While Calvin continued to work that evening, President Wolfkill came by and seeing him still plastering asked him: "What are you doing here working so late?" He answered that "There had been an excess batch of plaster made up, and rather than throw it away, I decided to miss supper and stay until the plaster was used." The president went home and had his wife prepare Calvin a delicious dinner. So amazed that Calvin possessed such concern, maturity, and industry, he showed his appreciation by inviting him to his home and sit at his table for a meal—and this at a time when the socio-political climate did not recommend or accept such association between blacks and whites. In fact, eating a meal with the president in his home came in stark contrast with the segregated policy a few yards away in the campus cafeteria. Ever mindful and appreciative for the brave hospitality decades into the future, yet Calvin's daily fare was to dine daily at a segregated table. It was the latter which caused him to say years later: "That's one thing in my life that embittered me. For that reason, Emmanuel Missionary College holds no warm spot in my heart. The very fact that I went from the south to the north, and I was told by people who were supposed to know that in those days there was no segregation in the north as it was in the south, and yet I had to sit at a segregated table every time I ate." Hats off to President Wolfkill who courageously refused to allow policy to override Christian hospitality in his home!

Calvin did not rush through his work assignment. He wanted his product to pass the scrutiny of the school authorities and always had in mind his need for further work that might be coming his way. Outstanding work would surely not go unnoticed. To his happiness, the business office reported that the plastering of the lower auditorium by Calvin exceeded in excellence that done in the upper chapel area by someone else. Whether in his scholarship or at his trade, his consistent fidelity and quality performance propelled him above the ordinary and paved the way for sure success.

Mission and Miracle

That he might put his classroom theory about ministry into practical application, Calvin frequently engaged in off-campus witnessing in 1928-29 among churches surrounding the Berrien Springs, Michigan, area. While I was recently sifting through his papers and files in 2016, I came upon his hand-written account of one of his student mission experiences. I had heard him relate the same episode around the family dinner table a time or two much later in his life, but to find that exact incident recorded in his own handwriting came as a treasure trove! Especially did two things touch me: first, I had no idea any such "document" existed and, secondly, I found his written portrayal laced with such drama and intrigue that I thought it so powerfully touching and engaging to share. Here it is:

> "Study at the college proceeded smoothly until a single miscalculation almost ruined my future. A company of believers in Southbend, Indiana, invited me to spend as many Sabbaths as I could with them. And as that invitation provided

opportunity to do some practice teaching and preaching, I accepted. A local teacher noting our progress invited me to help her with a Bible class she was conducting on Sunday evenings at a private home in Benton Harbor, Michigan. Again I was agreeable, and quickly that class gave promise of becoming quite fruitful in decision-making for Christ.

"Unhappy with that turn of events, the enemy of all Christian activity set about to destroy both the class and possibly me. On the evening when decisions seemed eminent [sic], I lingered a few moments longer than usual to assure success. Thankfully, my goal was gained, but that lingering threatened my return to the college that evening which experience also might have caused my dismissal from the institution.

"I rushed to put on my overcoat and rubbers and ran out to catch the last street car that would take me to the very last interurban train to reach the college that evening. As I stepped into four inches of snow and began running, that street-car which was a short block ahead pulled away! I ran my fastest, but that [street] car outran me and disappeared in the distance!

"Now, what am I to do? I had no money besides that resurved [sic] to pay for the streetcar and train tickets. I had no acquaintances in Benton Harbor except Bible Class members; and they were dismissed and dispersed. Weary and breathing hard from running in four inches of snow at night, I kept repeating what must I do? I stopped and prayed for help. Then thinking of nothing more, I resumed my walking in the snow-filled car tracks and turned around where I last saw that streetcar turn.

"Still praying, I looked and there against the street curve sat a large black limousine. The motor was running and exhaust smoke was coiling from twin pipes. The front seat was occupied by two husky black men dressed in black leather coats and caps. With a prayer and fear in my troubled heart I walked to that limousine and rapped on the driver's door. He turned and inquired softly: 'What is it?' Earnestly and sincerely I explained my predicament. His only response was: 'Get in.' Words never sounded sweeter! Quickly, I opened that huge back door and sat on a wide leather seat, then closed my eyes and prayed again: 'Thank you, dear God. Thank you, thank you, thank you.' Dear reader, this all sounds like a dream to me even now. But believe me, every word of it is real!

"The men sat talking softly each to the other for the full three miles to the train station, but they uttered not one word to me. And try as I did, I could not understand anything that they were saying. At times I wonder even now, why I did not or could not make conversation with them. I only remember that we passed the streetcar shortly, and I waved at it gleefully and with joy as we passed. Only heaven knows how wonderfully mystified I was with all that was happening.

"Reaching my destination, as quickly as I had entered that limozene [*sic*], just so quickly I opened the door and ran towards that waiting train; and with one foot on the first step I heard the words: 'You did not thank those men for bringing you here!' And never breaking my speed, I wheeled around and ran back those twenty or twenty-five yards to express my gratitude—but there was no limousine; it had disappeared completely! Quickly I looked in every possible direction, even upward! But that limousine was not to be seen! Dazed, bewildered and confused, I returned to the train and sat down. I tried to wonder what could possibly have happened, but my thinking apparatus seemed to have simply shut down. All that ever came to mind then, and even now, was Psalm 34:7 ['The angel of the LORD encampeth round about them that fear him, and delivereth them.']

"Had not that limousine enabled me to return to the college [EMC] that evening, no explanation given the authorities by me could have prevented my being expelled from the institution. My story, however truthful, would have made me the laughing stock of the campus. Who would have believed such a weird tale? Understanding how most humans think, I kept my experience to myself and divulged it to neither kindred, friend or foe for twelve years. To this day, that unique deliverance, as I still call it, was providential in every detail, and it is a cause for never ending praise and thanksgiving to the eternal God." ("Providences." Handwritten personal experiences by Calvin E. Moseley himself. Archives of Eva B. Dykes Library of Oakwood University)

Hiccups Along the Way

On another front, within the campus church at EMC, things did not pan out so well as in the home of the president. Social folkways and mores urged that a segregated Sabbath school class be organized. Calvin remembered that "They actually tried [to have] a teacher to inaugurate a black class for just the four of us or the three of us, and they wanted me to be the teacher. I refused to do it; and I wouldn't even stay on the campus on Sabbath. I went to South Bend, Indiana, so they wouldn't continue to ask me [and I could] escape having an all black Sabbath school class. Their idea for [having such a class was] 'well we have an all French class, we have a German class, we have a Spanish class, why not have a black class?' I retorted: 'Not a bit for me!' So we didn't do it." Half a century beyond his student days at EMC, he retired in Huntsville, Alabama. When Clara Peterson Rock (Archivist of Eva B. Dykes Library at Oakwood University) informed him that one of his EMC classmates (Mrs. Phenicie Skinner Thomas) was visiting the Huntsville area, her name prompted for him a reflection of "hard times" they and other blacks went through. Responding to Archivist Peterson's thought that his EMC experience contributed something to him, Calvin then offered this final redeeming assessment: "Yes, it made me make up my mind that if God would provide the opportunity I would stay there and live through that 'junk'—I call it 'junk' because it spoiled a lot of my pleasures and embittered my life a good deal. I made up my mind that I would want to be one to come back to this college [Oakwood] and encourage everybody else [to feel] that I could to go to that college [EMC] . . . and not have to endure what I went through. That's precisely the reason I stayed there, and I had to force myself to stay there. . . . I didn't enjoy it at all!" The antecedent of "it" here refers to separatist policies and practices based on race being far from enjoyable while the academic program proved very satisfactory.

Approaching the end of his final school term, Calvin lacked sufficient funds to graduate. Prayerfully, he ventured a request of Mr. Arms, business manager, to permit him to graduate with a promise to clear his financial debt when and if the Illinois Conference came through on its promise to employ him. Arrangement granted. In the summation of things, his overall experience at EMC provided quality preparation for ministry. Among Christian educators and students on northern as on southern campuses, there were varying degrees of tolerance and growth in race relations. This Alabama boy had begun his journey on the learning curve of deciphering relational veneers and seeing the glaring light of the facts of life. From there he would continue on his road of becoming.

rabBi
BESPEAKING

Nineteen-twenty nine. The stock market crashing. The Great Depression gripping the nation. Nineteen-twenty nine. Amid national economic disaster, Calvin Edwin Moseley, Jr. is graduating from Emmanuel Missionary College. The newly minted "minister" with his B.A. degree in Religion and History, however, steps into real life bearing an educational debt, a type of depression of its own. But that does not dampen his spirit and sense of accomplishment. After all, he has attained the highest ministerial degree the SDA church has to offer at the time. He feels fully equipped, at least theoretically, for pastoral-evangelistic service and well on his way toward speaking for God. Of all places selected for his inaugural pastorate by the Illinois Conference, a city not too distant from the Chicago area becomes his parish. Evanston, Illinois awaits him, and he looks forward to his maiden congregation. Something about being near Chicago appeals to him and tugs for his attention on a personal and social level. He thinks he knows why and will understand even better in days to come. Business before pleasure steers him for the moment, but inevitably as time goes by, business and pleasure will form for him a friendship. That which had been for Calvin the student a telescope peering into the future has suddenly become a microscope bringing to full view his ministerial map for the present and future.

Summer Scare

Allow here a look at a summer episode leading up to and influencing Calvin's readiness for his Evanston pastorate. He and his evangelism associates are the key characters. Implications emerge as to whether he would or would not graduate on time with his class. Elder L. H. Christian of the Illinois Conference invited Calvin once again to join Elder George E. Peters to do evangelism in Chicago. The invitation stemmed from a recommendation by Peters himself. Coming from such a widely noted and prolific evangelist meant a huge endorsement of Calvin. Peters had conducted similar meetings in Tampa, Florida in the early 1920's resulting in almost 250 baptisms. Brought to Chicago for similar expected results, Peters' divinely anointed preaching and leadership did bring about scores of baptized converts in the Windy City and inspired conference leaders and parishioners to move forward there quickly for a new church building. This summer of 1928 followed several previous Chicago crusades one or two of which Calvin had already assisted as a student. Conference leadership and Evangelist Peters had come to know the EMC student quite well, his sincerity, fidelity, dependability, integrity and evidence of ministerial gifts. Peters moved forward with characteristic precision and made plans to throw out the lifeline there once again and point souls to accept the God of heaven through Jesus Christ and the influence of the Holy Spirit.

Different from previous Chicago crusades, the 1928 evangelism team would include the assistance not only of Calvin but also his former Oakwood Junior College schoolmate, Emile Jarreau, both being joint caretakers of the tent and associates to the evangelist. Surprisingly, a curious thing happened to Calvin and Emile when a young man from New York needing a place to stay also became part of the crusade workforce on a temporary basis. To Calvin and Emile, this additional help came as a windfall; so they took advantage of it by asking the newcomer to watch the canvas pavilion while they took a breather and did "a bit of shopping" assuring him: "We will be back soon." Obviously, their plan went awry because while they were away, their helper fell asleep, which allowed someone to come along and steal all their clothing. Calvin himself had only the suit on his back except for another that lay between the two mattresses of his cot—their method for pressing their suits. A bit crude no doubt but their best alternative to the expensive professional cleaners. Such a method further enabled Calvin to save every dollar for his EMC tuition. Although he said nothing about their loss, his associate Emile reported their misfortune to Evangelist Peters who that very night made an appeal to the congregation to "help these two worthy young men." The response proved very generous for each of them and enabled Calvin to purchase "two suits"—one a blue serge. The summer's end found him far better off than its beginning and permitting him to return to Emmanuel Missionary College with a wardrobe containing a "special suit for Sabbath." The "blue serge" suit, however, he saved for graduation and kept it ready for the 1929 Commencement. certainly, the pattern was being set for becoming an equipped and attired spokesperson for the gospel of Jesus Christ.

Immediately following graduation but before full-time pastoring, he returned home to spend two weeks with his mother and father. There his dad, Calvin, Sr., was plying his usual plastering trade trying to make ends meet but apparently not sufficiently to navigate threatening waves of the depression. Mother Lillie Belle worked as a midwife, but instead of money she received what the people could avoid: chickens, eggs, calves, and vegetables which kept mom and dad Moseley from going into the bread line. When Calvin, Jr. began his pastoral duties in 1929 and accrued a salary, he sent a portion of his earnings back home to his parents monthly for two years. This he said "kept them out of the bread line. Otherwise they would have been in the bread line like thousands of blacks and almost an equal number of whites." He did this noble gesture for his parents with an entry-level pastoral salary of "twenty-one dollars and a half a week," which "worked up to twenty-four dollars and a half over a period of about three years."

Reminiscing about this farther down life's road in retirement fifty years later, he contrasted day-to-day life as a pastor against day-to-day life as an Oakwood teacher: "When I came to Oakwood [after years of pastoring] I received a cut in my salary. It dropped from twenty-four to twenty-two fifty." The cost of living on campus, nonetheless, did prove less expensive than living in the city and, fortunately, afforded opportunities for personal gardening of fruits and vegetables. "The effects of depression was [*sic*] still being felt, and jobs were hard to come by and scarce, and there was not an abundance of money out there. But . . . on the grounds [Oakwood campus following his years pastoring churches] we had a good garden. There was a fine dairy here, and they grew produce in great abundance; so everything was reasonable. Actually the twenty-two fifty [Oakwood salary] went farther than the twenty-four [pastoral salary]." Ah, the illusiveness of lucre, but it's only a medium of exchange.

Evanston Evangelist, Evanston Pastor

After two weeks with parents in Mississippi following graduation from EMC in 1929, Calvin returned to Illinois to serve with Elder Peters in summer evangelism this time in the city of Evanston itself, a mere hop, skip and jump from Chicago. By now, the Peters-Moseley team had become a familiar billing for several of these soul-winning exploits. In the meantime, the largest black SDA congregation in America (the Ephesus Church in Harlem, New York) shepherded by Elder J. K. Humphrey was facing a crisis. Under his leadership, Ephesus tilted toward pulling away from the parent denominational body. While in the middle of his own Evanston evangelistic effort, Elder Peters was sent into the cauldron of boiling apostasy in New York to calm the troubled waters. The need forced him to leave the Evanston meeting with only about two or three weeks remaining for completion. Unfinished business involved "binding off" the Evanston evangelistic program and organizing the new converts into a functional worship body.

Elder Peters' steadying voice was commissioned to New York to salvage what he could from the situation there and try to recover pieces of a splintered church influenced by Humphrey. Despite his otherwise progressive and commendable leadership, Humphrey tended more and more away from the organized SDA denomination. When Peters began devoting less time in Evanston and more time in New York, the Evanston meetings were shortened to three nights each week with Peters returning for one night and then establishing permanent residence in New York. Emile Jarreau, himself a teacher (who had spent a prior summer as co-associate with Moseley to Elder Peters in a Chicago meeting), returned to his school as did a third associate. This left no one but the newly appointed pastor/leader for Evanston to become instantly the Evanston evangelist with a lone Bible worker. Moseley had never had previous experience doing solo planning, conducting, and bespeaking for an evangelistic crusade; nevertheless, under the providence of God he completed the meetings. "The Spirit of God came upon me in such power that enabled me to preach as I had never preached before," he subsequently stated. Persons attending the gatherings voiced the same sentiment. Moseley concluded the meetings appropriately.

Not very long after Moseley brought the Evanston meetings to a close with thirty-five new members baptized, Elder Peters found his way back from New York for the organization of the first Evanston, Illinois church. One can imagine that his appreciation for Moseley's backup leadership sparked his motivation for being present at the formal introduction of Moseley to his first pastorate in 1930. As for Moseley himself, a flashback out of the past jogged his memory about a solemn vow he made to God while studying at Oakwood Junior College. Sitting in the Bible class of W. L. H. Baker and seeking to dodge the call to ministry because of fear and unable to silence the inner voice of the Holy Spirit, he had prayed: "Lord, I make You a promise to make sure You want me to preach. If You will arrange affairs in my life so that I will become the pastor of a brand *new church that is newly organized*, if You will do that for me, I will take that as proof You really want me to preach." Moseley long desired to grow in experience with new believers. Like presto! To the very letter, that prayer was being answered right there before his very eyes. The baptized converts would be organized into the new Evanston church, and with nothing short of praise and gratitude, Moseley recaptured the spirit of that vow made to God during student days at Oakwood. Present at this pastoral installation with Elder Peters was Elder Herbert Green, pastor of the Shiloh Church in Chicago. Actually, Moseley was being ordained the First Elder and leader of the Evanston congregation with pastoral responsibilities. While he bowed on his knees amid prayers and blessings of the officiants Peters and Green, like a thunderbolt out of the blue that vow again visited his mind. Deep within his spirit, he witnessed vow and fulfillment holding hands side by side and kissing each other.

Let us insert at this point another interesting dimension of his Evanston experience that related to his education. When Moseley graduated from Emmanuel Missionary College in 1929, his major instructor there, Cris P. Soyasen, had encouraged him to continue his education by attending graduate school. After giving the idea some thought and recommended for admission by Percy Christian (son of L. H. Christian, President of the Illinois Conference), he decided on advanced studies in history at Northwestern University which happened to be right there in Evanston. Due to economic pressures by the national depression, Moseley attended only for a short time.

At any rate, Moseley remained in Evanston one and one half years. Nurturing the saints there, in his opinion, yielded a mixed bag of joy and sorrow—the former from sheer delight of serving in the zone of God's will, the latter from disappointment that not one additional soul came into the church through baptism. He could not see momentarily the multiplied thousands he would be blessed to invite over time to the foot of the cross of Jesus Christ through his own preaching, teaching, and witnessing as well as through students he would prepare for gospel ministry.

You might say Evanston amounted to "post graduate" field work. Every Sabbath after preaching at his church, Moseley had to go to Chicago to be debriefed by Elder Green at Shiloh who had become his supervisor and mentor. Green being a most affable and jovial person with a very pleasant disposition, their confab took place in a relaxed and comfortable atmosphere. Invariably, Green would get the conversation going with: "Brother Moseley, what did you preach about today?" Moseley would tell him the sermon title, and Greed would lightheartedly throw his head back with a hearty laugh. On one Sabbath afternoon, his laughter seemed to carry a special meaning which prompted Moseley to ask him: "What are you laughing about, Elder?" Green responded: "Would you believe it, I preached about the same thing this morning?" Because this coincidence happened a number of times, the young Evanston pastor convinced himself to consider it more than coincidence and deemed it valid basis for encouragement. God had to be smiling, he thought, on his development and progress in honing his skills for ministry.

Springfield, Illinois: a Breather and a Breakthrough

Particularly one person, a Holiness Church pastor, seemed interested in the gospel preached by Moseley in Evanston; but he would not be baptized. The experience left the optimistic preacher disappointed and a bit shaken. His extremity, however, met divine opportunity when invited to Springfield, Illinois to conduct a Week of Prayer and revival. At first the invite appeared little different from his lean church growth experience in Evanston when informed that the congregation totaled sixteen members, half of them elderly, some confined to bed, and few could attend church on a regular basis. Nevertheless, Moseley's brief pastoral tenure made him no stranger to proverbial "hard trials and great tribulations." Feeling by now he had accrued some expertise for tough assignments, he proceeded with a will to work.

The Week of Prayer and Revival series consisted of nine sermons. During that week, the Holy Spirit gave him nine decisions, averaging one soul each night, even though he made only two direct appeals for joining the church. Returning to Evanston, Moseley attended the Illinois Conference Workers' Meeting held in Chicago where each pastor and evangelist was required to give a report of soul-winning endeavors for Jesus Christ. To his surprise, he had the best record of all the young pastor evangelists. Probably the challenge of Spingfield at the time cannot be fully appreciated except against the backdrop of an unnamed leading and experienced evangelist who the next summer was provided with budget, workers, and facilities and yet found barriers to "success" almost insurmountable. Nonetheless, following that summer Moseley and another young pastor, D. J. Dixon, were asked to return to Springfield and conduct another evangelistic crusade. Among the younger pastors, they were the only ones not assigned to assist a more experienced pastor-evangelist. Moseley's pointing this out to the brethren brought only smiles. The Moseley-Dixon team had no alternative but to forward march into the fray. Their equipment consisted of a sixty-foot circle tent (giving a "merry-go-round" effect) and enough money to pay for erecting the tent. Pianist and other needed workers would have to be paid from the offerings which were nonexistent during the planning and preparation stage. Clearly, this evangelistic journey in Springfield would have to start "by faith and not by sight."

How did the Moseley-Dixon meetings come out in the end? They preached for six weeks and were blessed with thirty-five decisions for Jesus Christ in the setting of Seventh-day Adventism. As a matter of fact, the resounding report of baptisms was received so joyfully by conference leaders that Calvin Moseley and D. J. Dixon were crowned with the assignment of conducting another meeting in Springfield that same summer after only two week's rest and recuperation. So for another several weeks they were at it again—throwing out the lifeline for souls. Moseley was unaware of how near he came to exhaustion until the final week of the evangelistic campaign. He could hardly speak above conversational tones which kept him praying to God for divine aid. Faith went to work for the Moseley-Dixon duo and yielded an additional thirty-three decisions to accept Jesus Christ as personal Saviour and commit to the Bible as the word of God. Upon learning of the state of Moseley's health, the conference president offered him a two weeks' vacation. Being a person deeply rooted in family, he set his face toward Jackson, Mississippi to see his beloved parents, swung by Oakwood Junior College for "precious memories," and then headed back to Springfield, Illinois. After baptizing the new converts there, he was asked to remain as resident pastor of the growing congregation, a people relishing their first love for Christ and the great advent message. As for Pastor Moseley, word was spreading fast and far that his fruitful ministry indeed bespoke of his call to Christian service.

Unfinished Business

Remember the Oakwood quartet referred to earlier whose itinerary took in Chicago around 1925 or 1926? Do you recall one of the singers, Calvin Moseley, Jr., being introduced to an attractive "Miss Slater?" Recapturing the experience he would remark: "After that trip, I kept her in memory . . . . When I got in the ministry I inquired about her." Actually, Calvin had restrained any direct further contact with Harriet Frances Slater from the time of his Oakwood quartet days until after graduating from Emmanuel

Missionary College, where his roommate happened to be her boyfriend. Graduating from EMC in 1929 and entering the ministry in 1930, he continued thinking about the Chicago mademoiselle, making inquiries about her but nothing more. After a four or five year stretch since first being introduced to her about 1926 during his Oakwood Jubilee Quartet tour through Chicago, the moment of truth was drawing nigh.

You might say several baby steps brought them closer into each other's presence before the giant leap of serious business. Both were invited to a church member's home for dinner while he was a pastor, but the conversation remained casual at best. Other dinners followed that brought them into one another's company from several homes including that of the Slaters'. Sometime later, unrelated to the sequence of invited dinners but probably due more to his own cooking, he contracted a condition that greatly affected his digestion and causing him to go to the Hinsdale Sanitarium and Hospital for diagnosis and treatment. While riding on the train from Evanston to Hinsdale, he came to a small station stop and to his happy surprise Harriet Slater also boarded the train on her way to nurse training at the Hinsdale Hospital. Passing by she tapped him on the shoulder, smiled and said: "Hello." Moseley responded: "Hello, I did not know you were here. Where are you going?" "I'm going to the hospital," Harriet replied and inquired: "Where are you going?" Moseley answered: "I'm going to the hospital also." She then sat down beside him. At some point she curiously said: "You haven't married yet!" He answered: "No-o! Girls are kinda few—all the best of them and all the good ones are taken . . . like you and a few of the rest of them!" To that Moseley recalled that she said: "Oh-o" and smiled and let him know she and the other young man [his former EMC roommate] had severed their connection. "I made up my mind," he decided, "that I would make a connection, and so we did!" No binding commitment took place immediately, only a decision in his heart that opportunity was knocking at his door, and he determined to answer. Preparing to leave at her train stop, Harriet waved and smiled. He was convinced that providence brought them together that day pointing to better days ahead. It all led to seeds being sown which sooner than later would bud, grow, and blossom into a beautiful, fragrant flower. Before very long, Calvin Moseley and Harriet Slater engaged themselves to be married.

Best Laid Plans

Let us bear in mind that these starry-eyed motions for marriage were being made in the early 1930's during the Great Depression, a time of severe economic drought. The unwelcomed but steady tread of unemployment stepped into the path of the pastor of the Springfield, Illinois church; and because of staff retrenchment, Moseley as quick as snapping his finger became an unemployed minister which threatened plans for marriage. What would he do next? What could he do with this untimely dilemma?

Those whom God calls he also enables. Pastor Moseley went to his church and informed them of his new status. The congregation asked pensively: "What are you going to do?" He replied in typical thoughtful and premeditated Moseley style: "I believed I have figured it out. . . . This is what I have decided. I was saving some money to get married, and I made up my mind that I will stay here until I use it all up. I earned it serving God here in this church, and I'll stay here and use it until it's all gone, and I'll leave it in God's hands. I am still a plasterer, and I know how to work. I can still make a living."

Meanwhile, a new phase of administrative outreach for the black community had been organized at this time across the North American Division particularly in areas where the black population was enormous. At the time, blacks were the nation's largest minority at 11,891,143. To oversee and develop the church work among blacks in the state of Missouri, an ethnic leader was chosen named Elder Thomas Allison, a man of great ability, forceful appearance, and well known for his preaching, singing, and expertise at the piano.

About a week into unemployment, Pastor Moseley found himself out in his landlady's backyard forking up her garden just for exercise. It was too early for planting. Glancing upward, to his surprise, he saw Elder Allison approaching. Quite startled, Moseley said: "What are you doing here?" "I've come for you," responded Allison. "Come for me," questioned Moseley." "What do you mean by that?" "Well," Allison replied, "you don't have a job; I heard about it, and I have a job for you. So, I've come for you." Circumstances surrounding this visit by Elder Allison deeply convinced Moseley that divine providence moved mightily to bring it about. Moseley had been pastoring and still living in the Illinois Conference while Elder Allison was serving in the Missouri Conference. They were acquainted with each other only casually with no correspondence or communication between them, and Moseley had put out no feelers. He had resigned himself to the *modus operandi* of using his "hawk and trowel" as a plasterer and wait upon the Lord. Understandably, to this young pastor "without portfolio," Allison was a God-send and brought to mind that Moseley had been waiting prayerfuly and was now experiencing Isaiah 40:3: "They that wait upon the Lord shall renew their strength; they shall mount up with wings as eagles; they shall run and not be weary; and they shall walk, and not faint." (Isaiah 40:31)

Although good news from Elder Allison brought exhilarating happiness and satisfaction, Moseley felt in the depths of his joyous emotions a pang of sadness, a tinge of angst, because he remembered promising his former congregation that "I will stay with you for six months, and then I will have to go." Explaining his new dilemma to Elder Allison, he asked: "What shall I do? I cannot just tell them you have come for me, and I must leave. You will have to straighten this out." Elder Allison replied: "All right, I will straighten it out."

Notice was sent out to all the Springfield church members inviting them to come to a special meeting. Elder Allison explained the matter, informing the congregation of the conditions that brought on the termination of several workers [in Illinois Conference] not to Pastor Moseley only. In spite of the clarity and logic of the move, the saints were "practically up in arms." Like family they had seen him develop from a "fledgling intern" into a dynamic and self-composed pastor-evangelist. Though their pastor for a relatively short period, he had grown into their hearts and they into his. Yet he was now being offered a timely privilege to become employed again though by another conference [Missouri] in response to the counsel and endorsement of Elder Allison. The approved plan beckoned Moseley to St. Louis, a church with a more urgent need and a larger responsibility. It was clearly evident that Moseley's capability and growth patterns commended him to such a pastoral charge. Nevertheless, the Springfield church refused to give up their pastor without a struggle nor were the cords binding him so dearly to their hearts to be loosened so easily. He himself felt a huge reluctance to the idea of leaving a group of worshipers who had responded so favorably to his shepherd leadership, and his promise to remain with them several more months did not lend itself to a smooth transition. Stormy waves of emotion began breaking over the congregation who wept profusely.

Moseley could not bear this scene untouched and created another wave when he exclaimed to Elder Allison: "Wait a minute, brother. This is not the way to do it. I don't have to go." Elder Allison intervened immediately saying: "Now just a moment, Elder Moseley, let me manage this." Eventually, he was able to calm the troubled waters and get the congregation to understand the situation and "agree" to Moseley's departure. However, they were not letting go without some consideration for themselves by asking:

"But what are we going to do? You are taking our minister, and he told us he was staying longer." Allison answered: "I will speak to the Illinois Conference president and ask him to send someone here periodically to minister to you. Elder Owen Troy of the Shiloh Church in Chicago has a lot of help. In the meantime, St. Louis is a large field and a large city church, and their minister soon will be leaving."

Soon thereafter, Elder Allison took Moseley to St. Louis and introduced him as their new minister in 1931 where he served until 1934. To the utter surprise of the new pastor, he had been cast, as it were, into another tempestuous sea even more turbulent than the one he just left. In common parlance, he went from the frying pay into the fire. Before he could even select a sermon text or preach one sermon in St. Louis, he landed on a church runway headed for dissension, divisiveness and a threat to split. God's grace working through Moseley's maturing pastoral leadership, however, was sufficient to prevent the worst.

Cupid's Call and More

Over a three year period since his graduation from Emmanuel Missionary College, pastoral skills of Calvin Moseley grew progressively better beginning with his initiation in the windy city of Chicago, 1929. From there his ministerial gifts bore a maturity which recommended him to Evanston, Illinois then Springfield, Illinois and eventually, in 1931, St. Louis, Missouri while also supervising the colored work for the state of Missouri. While faithfully answering the call of these churches, nonetheless, Moseley increasingly found his heart responding to love's call for companionship. All along he had been thinking often about the grand young lady named Harriet of the Shiloh Church in Chicago and had periodically conversed with her while also attending several dinners arranged by church members to bring them together. Occasionally, he had also been invited to dinner at the home of his lady of interest hosted by her mother, Mrs. Harriet Slater Hall. More than likely his accepting the call to St. Louis brought with it a nervous sense of distance further away from Chicago and especially from Harriet Frances Slater. Having arrived in St. Louis during his third year of pastoring and proclamation of the gospel, more than ever before, he heard the clarion call of Genesis 2:18: "The Lord God said, 'It is not good for the man to be alone. I will make a helper suitable for him." (NIV)

On June 15, 1933, Calvin Edwin Moseley, Jr. and Harriet Frances Slater were married in Shiloh, her home church. According to *The Acorn* (student paper by Oakwood Jr. College; August, 1933), one of the local newspapers, *The Chicago Defender*, reported an audience of nine-hundred witnesses to the wedding conducted by Elder Owen A. Troy, pastor of Shiloh. The bridal party included Eric Dillett, Emile Jarreau (father of Al Jarreau, decades later to become a famous show business musican), H. T. Saulter, George Murphy, Fred Slater (brother of the bride), Rose Hemsley, and Ruth Frazier, Joseph F. Dent, D. W. Crowe, and Mrs. Ruby Troy. Two beautiful flower girls adorned the ceremony: Marian Blevins (cousin to the bride) and Rose Marie Vaughn (decades later the bride of Robert H. Carter, pastor and administrator). Also in attendance were Oakwood Junior College students past and present including Marie Blanks, Irene Blanchard, and Ruby Brown along with prospective students for the ensuing year. Queen of all visitors, Mrs. Lillie Belle Dixon Moseley (mother of the groom) came all the way from Mississippi for the occasion. Following a brief honeymoon in Springfield, Illinois, the couple headed for St Louis, Missouri, as Pastor and First Lady of the church there. Just recently, 2016, a retired staff of Oakwood University, Mrs. Lovey Davis Verdun, related to me that she recalls as a little girl in the St. Louis church in 1933 that her pastor, Calvin Moseley, "left to go to Chicago and came back with a wife."

Homing and the Call to Return

Pastoring the Berean Church in St. Louis was short-lived (1931-1934) though packed with signal progress in church nurturing, soul winning, and ministerial peer leadership. While there, Moseley ministered also in the neighboring state of Kansas where he baptized Mr. and Mrs. Frank W. Hale, Sr. and son, Frank, II, the latter who became president of Oakwood University (1966-71). Moseley proved himself a pastor who could preach, a preacher who could pastor, a pastor who could lead, a pastor who could follow. So when 1934 arrived, only two years after the historic presidential change taken place on the campus of Oakwood Junior College, he followed his heart and accepted the invitation to join the Oakwood faculty and become integral to the transformational campus with its first black president, James L. Moran. In the face of all white faculty resigning, President Moran himself must have been staring at panic-ville to find competent replacements among the Oakwood faculty so that instruction might continue confidently and on schedule.

So the newly wed pastor of only one year, so accustomed to new assignments and new opportunities, heard the call of President Moran to bring his consecrated competence to a most crucial position, namely, Head of the Bible Department. Unlike the Deuteronomic waiver that "if a man has recently married, he must not be sent to war or have any other duty laid on him. For one year he is to be free to stay at home and bring happiness to the wife he has married" (Deut. 24:5), Moseley the "recently married" headed instead for the challenge awaiting him. President Moran and others who recommended Moseley to return to Oakwood Junior College thought he embodied a rich and attractive mixture of formal education and successful pastoral experience, the former being a B.A. degree representing the highest academic preparation for ministers within the SDA denomination at the time and the latter comprising a very productive and successful ministry albeit brief. Add to

Pencil portrait of Calvin Edwin Moseley Jr. by Oakwood University student Turner Battle, 1946

Lillie Bell (Dixon) and Calvin E. Moseley Sr., parents of Calvin Jr. and Ernest

Calvin Jr., student trumpet player in Jackson State College Band (front row, sixth from right), 1923

Calvin Jr., senior student at Oakwood Junior College, 1927

Oakwood Jubilee Quartet (clockwise from bottom right): Calvin Jr., Frank Peterson, John Wagner, Charles Salisbury, 1924–25

Oakwood Glee Club singers: Calvin Jr., directing (front row left), 1925

Ernest Moseley in Oakwood Quartet (L–R): Emile Jarreau, Otis Edwards, Harvey Kibble, Ernest Moseley, 1927

Illinois Conference workers (back row, far left): Calvin Moseley Jr.

Certificate of Ordination/Missouri Conference, Calvin Jr

Graduating class, Hinsdale Hospital (far right, second from top): Harriet Slater, future wife of Calvin Moseley Jr.; (far left, second from top): Ruth Frazier, future teacher of Oakwood.

Harriet Slater engagement photo for Calvin Jr., 1931

Wedding of Harriet Slater and Calvin Moseley Jr., 1933

Oak Hill Cemetery, Battle Creek, MI, gravesite of abolitionist Sojourner Truth (first left: Owen Troy Sr.; first right: Calvin Moseley Jr.; fourth from Moseley: Wilbert Forde), c. 1933

James Moran, first black president of Oakwood College, the one who invited Moseley Jr. to join faculty, 1934

Moseley (L) with his religion faculty: Clarence Richards and Ernest Rogers, mid-1940's

John Beale, later addition to religion faculty

Moseley (standing) confers with Otis B. Edwards (academic dean) and Frank L. Peterson (president) of Oakwood College

President Peterson (successor to James Moran) and Mrs. Bessie Peterson

(L–R): Moseley Jr., Mrs. Moseley, and her brother Elder Fred Slater, late 1930's

Harriet Slater Hall with son-in-law, Calvin Moseley Jr.

Moseley Jr. and wife, Harriet Frances, and two daughters (L–R): Harriet Ann and baby Barbara Jean

Moseleys at family worship (L–R): father, sisters Barbara and Harriet, and mother

Brothers: Calvin Jr. and Ernest Moseley

Regional presidents visiting the Oakwood campus (L–R): H. R. Murphy, J. Wagner Sr., L. Bland, H. Singleton, J. G. Dasent, 1946

Mother Lillie Belle and father Calvin Moseley Sr. (rear center); their son Ernest and wife Ethel (rear left); Harriet and Calvin Jr. (rear right); Ernest Jr., Barbara, Eddie, Harriet Ann (second row, L–R); Lillie Belle and Frances (front, L–R), 1949

Moseley Jr. and a homiletics and preaching class at Oakwood, late 1940's

Moseley (front center) and the Alabama Singers of Oakwood College, 1950

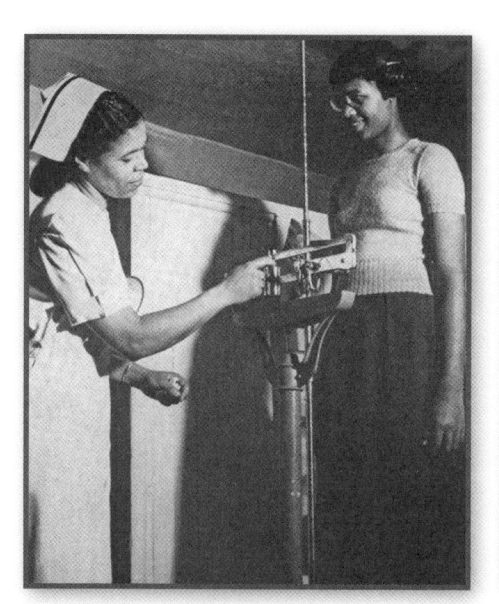

Mrs. Harriet Moseley, campus nurse, at Oakwood College

Eva B. Dykes, English and literature teacher and first PhD on Oakwood faculty, 1944–45

Board of Trustees, Oakwood College, 1946

Kappa Mu Delta, student men of excellence, 1951

Moseley Jr. in typical contemplation

Ministerial Seminary (later became The Forum) for weekly Friday evening student praxis in preaching and discussions. Sponsor: Moseley, seated far right

Senior ministerial students, 1951, construct and dedicate campus bell tower in honor of Elder Moseley

W. H. Branson, General Conference president, 1950–54

R. R. Figuhr, General Conference president, 1954–1966

W. H. Green, first black to head Regional Department of General Conference (1918–28)

George E. Peters, successor to W. H. Green, Regional Department of General Conference (1929f., 1941f., and 1951)

Speakers for Ministerial Council (L–R): T. Carcich, C. E. Moseley Jr., R. R. Hegstad, R. H. Pierson, W. W. Fordham, N. R. Dower, R. R. Bietz, N. C. Wilson, 1970

H. D. Singleton and C. E. Moseley Jr. at General Conference session, 1985, New Orleans, LA

(L–R): F. L. Peterson, VP Richard Nixon, C. E. Moseley Jr., and Mrs. H. Reid greet at conference for religious leaders, Washington, DC

Moseley delivering a spirited devotional at the General Conference, 1954

British Guiana ordination (1965); Moseley front center

Moseley preaching in an evangelistic meeting

Moseley proclaiming the gospel

Moseley declaring the Word

Moseley appealing for decision

Moseley rejoicing at the response

Moseley speaking for church groundbreaking, Miami, FL, 1962

Mervyn and Barbara, fiancés at their wedding shower

Barbara Moseley and father, Elder Moseley, strolling toward the moment

(L–R center): Wedding: Barbara Warren and husband, Mervyn, become one, June 14, 1959, First SDA Church, Washington, DC

(L–R center): Wedding: Harriet Ann and husband, Donald, become one, August 1961, First SDA Church, Washington, DC

Ted N. C. Wilson, president, General Conference of SDA, 2010 to present

Dan Jackson, president, North American Division, 2017

Calvin Rock, OU president, who invited Moseley back to the Oakwood classroom after his 1971 retirement from the General Conference

Elder Moseley, retired, views pastoral photos on the OU Church wall where he himself is the first African American to serve, 1934–51

Leslie Pollard, current president, Oakwood University, 2017

Dedrick Blue, current dean of the School of Religion, Oakwood University, 2017

Carlton Byrd, current pastor of the OU Church, 2017

Melwyn A. "Bob" Mounter, first assigned assoc. pastor, OU Church, under E. C. Ward, 1982

A homiletics/preaching class at OU by Moseley right after retirement from GC, 1973

Elder Calvin E. Moseley upon return to OU, 1972

A reunion of past and present Male Chorus singers directed by Moseley, c. 1970's

Elder Moseley directing another of his choral groups, 1974

C. D. Brooks, E. E. Cleveland, and C. E. Bradford, former students of Moseley and after whom the OU Bradford-Cleveland-Brooks Leadership Center was named, 2007

Gardner Taylor and Calvin Moseley chat after the Concord Baptist Church pastor delivers a sermon at Oakwood, c.1973

Mervyn Warren, Barry Black (chaplain, US Senate), and Auldwin Humphrey share precious moment with the "Rabbi"

Successive chairpersons of the School of Religion from 1934 to 1998. C. E. Moseley Jr. (front center); C. T. Richards (second row, right); M. A. Warren (second row, left); B. F. Reaves Sr. (last row, right); J. H. Melancon (last row, left)

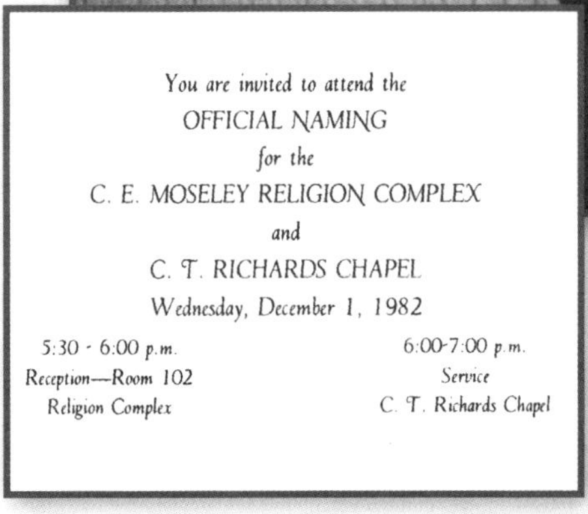

Elder Moseley standing by the instructional facility bearing his name

You are invited to attend the
OFFICIAL NAMING
for the
C. E. MOSELEY RELIGION COMPLEX
and
C. T. RICHARDS CHAPEL
Wednesday, December 1, 1982

5:30 - 6:00 p.m.   6:00-7:00 p.m.
Reception—Room 102   Service
Religion Complex   C. T. Richards Chapel

Program naming new religion building the C. E. Moseley Religion Complex and the worship room the C. T. Richards Chapel

The Rabbi relaxing by the fireplace    *Keeping in touch with his trumpet*

Always ready for a good laugh

Never far away from his garden

Beauty in nature reflects a beautiful God

Calvin and Harriet Moseley in their prime

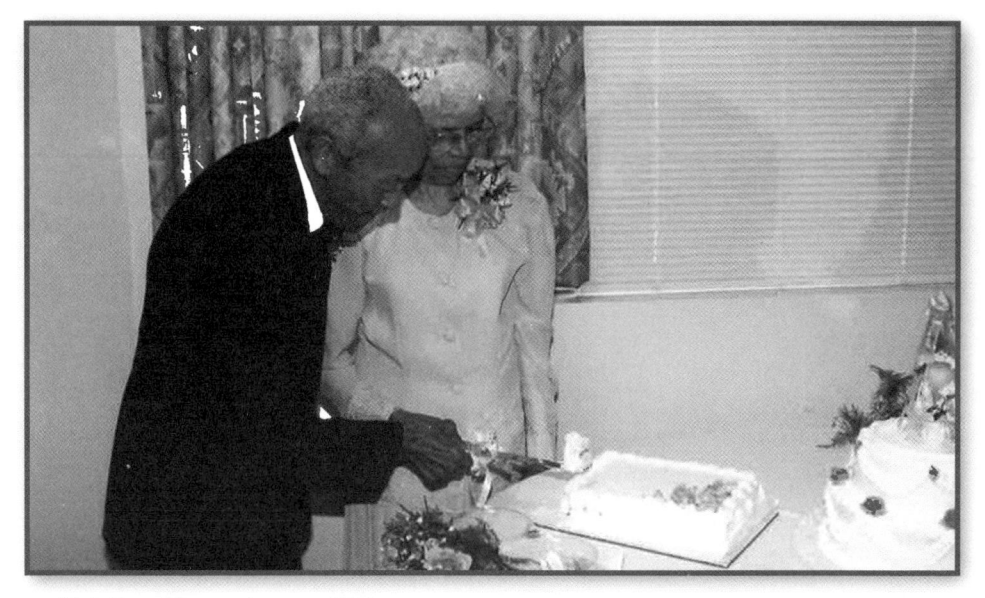

Sixtieth wedding anniversary, 1993

Family for sixtieth wedding anniversary with Elder and Mrs. Moseley seated front row center

Older Moseley daughter, Harriet Ann Keith (front center) with her family: Lori (second row, left); Karmen (second row, right); husband Donald (back, center)

Moseley grandchildren through daughter Barbara: Shana; Mervyn E.; Karis (front L–R); Elder and Mrs. Moseley seated (second row); Roberta Fields, mother of Mervyn A.; her son; Barbara (back row L–R)

Younger Moseley daughter, Barbara Jean Warren (second row, right behind her shortest grandchild, Mikey) with her family: husband, Mervyn, to her immediate left). The others include one son, two daughters, two sons-in-law, five granddaughters, and two grandsons (one granddaughter not in photo)

"Rabbi" Moseley and son-in-law Mervyn take a stroll through School of Religion hallway, a program that both of them were privileged to chair in their time

Pencil portrait of Calvin Edwin Moseley Jr. by Oakwood University student Johnny Mack, 1980

A few journal covers and pages celebrating the life and legacy of Calvin Edwin Moseley Jr.

this dual attraction resumé a varied background comprising a) his education at five noted institutions (Tuskegee Institute, Jackson College, Oakwood Junior College, and Emmanuel Missionary College [now Andrews University]), and Union College; b) his musical expertise; c) his experience in plastering (an industrial skill he continued to practice as needed even while pastoring); and d) his being an Oakwood alumnus. Quite probably, such a unique package of competences for the Huntsville school would have been rare and scarce if not generally unavailable among blacks in 1934. At any rate, Moseley once again listened to the voice of service and answered the call to duty.

He would be in for a surprise thinking his Oakwood appointment limited itself to teaching Bible. In fact, a string of surprises awaited him. With the new academic environment came the spawning of many fresh opportunities for bespeaking the Kingdom of God.

One Plus Two Equals . . .

To the amazement of the new young Bible teacher, almost in no time flat when his feet landed on the Oakwood grounds, he learned for the first time that his invitation to one position had multiplied to wearing three hats: Head of Bible Department, Dean of Men, and pastor of the campus church. No doubt the following scripture echoed in his mind many times: "I write to you, young men, because you are strong." (1 John 2:14, NIV) This being only the second year of J. L. Moran's presidency along with his being the first black in that position at Oakwood Junior College beginning 1932, Moseley found himself in the throes of a developing and re-organizing time behind the flight of all the white teachers and the scrambling to locate and engage qualified teachers black or white. (For example, curiously, the student paper, *The Acorn*, later named *The Spreading Oak*, published in its March 1934 issue that the Oakwood school board "voted to invite Elder O. A. Troy to unite with the faculty as head of the Department of Theology." Apparently, something ensued which prevented the vote from materializing inasmuch as that same year Calvin Moseley accepted the invitation to the position.) At any rate, for the burgeoning Moran team, a new day was dawning, and the sun would brighten the path of Moseley to contribute to the essence of the Oakwood dream.

Moseley spent his initial service time at Oakwood Junior College in 1934 without his wife, Harriet. Expectant with her first daughter, she remained with her mother in Chicago until the arrival of baby Harriet Ann at Hinsdale Sanitarium on January 7, 1935, the identical month and day as the birth of her father. When mother and daughter finally arrived at Oakwood, they joined him in Henderson Hall where he served as Dean of Men. Years into the future, he was interviewed by Archivist Clara Rock during his retirement in 1974: "How did your wife accept the . . . living conditions at Henderson Hall?" Professor Moseley responded: "Well, I actually must say we were so enamored one with the other in those early days that as far as I can remember she didn't complain seriously. The main thing . . . I think that interfered with her happiness if you'd call it that, was the fact that when I came down first I came alone. She was in Chicago because we were expecting Harriet Ann, and I didn't see her for about three months . . . 'til Harriet Ann came, and she brought Harriet Ann [to Oakwood] . . . and the noises would sometime [be disturbing]. . . . The boys in the dormitory would wake up the baby and . . . that was about the only thing that I ever heard her express any annoyance . . . ." (Interview of Elder C. E. Moseley by Clara P. Rock, Archivist, Eva B. Dykes Library, Oakwood College, February 3, 1974) An article entitled "Do You Want to Meet the Faculty" in the student paper introduced two new deans: Miss Julia Baugh of the women's dorm and Elder Moseley of the men's dorm, both graduates of Emmanuel Missionary College (now Andrews University). After presenting Moseley as "also the head of the Department of Biblical Instruction, in which capacity he has classes in Old Testament History, Advanced Bible Doctrines, and Homiletics," he is further called "Our musical dean." The feature continues that: "Elder Moseley is a talented artist on the cornet, having played it since being eighteen years of age. He has played in a number of bands and orchestras, including those of Tuskegee and Oakwood. While at Tuskegee, it was his duty to blow taps every night." (*The Acorn*, Oakwood Junior College, February, 1935, p. 5) And it would follow that the multi-talented and endowed would likewise be privileged with multi-assignments. To whom much is given, much is required. So to further equip himself to meet expanding responsibilities at Oakwood, he pursued graduate studies and by 1944 earned the M.A. degree from the Seventh-day Adventist Seminary while already engaged in writing articles for the *Message Magazine*, other denominational periodicals, and the publication of a book entitled *The Lord's Day*.

Bespeaking a Distinctive Note

Truth to tell, by the time theory joined hands with practicality in class assignments, Moseley did what most department heads do. He grabbed the bull by the horns, and he himself covered those courses for which other teachers were not available. So in addition to his official classes mentioned above, he taught also Daniel and the Revelation plus a class for the academy (high school) level. The plot thickens when you understand that his portfolio further comprised the supervision of three extern outlets for pastoral and evangelistic involvement for ministerial students in training, namely: 1) The Ministerial Seminar, a student club which met each Friday evening for discussions, presentations, and mock services of the church (in later decades the name of the seminar was changed and is known today as "The Forum" which has spanned the decades and continues to convene every Friday evening on the Oakwood University campus without a single hiatus since the 1930's when Elder Moseley first started it some seventy-five years ago); 2) The

Oakwood College Church, which he served as pastor for the entire campus and provided another platform for student participation; and 3) Supervising student externship arrangements among community churches.

Remember his love for music? His own earlier student days at Tuskegee, Jackson College, and at Oakwood Junior College during the 1920's? It became only natural and maybe even expected that he could not let heavy teaching loads prevent him from finding energy for extra-curricula like directing a traveling male chorus. The singing group would serve at least two purposes: Allow Moseley to feed his own deep love for music and also continue the timeless and most fruitful tradition of institutional recruitment through utilizing the singing talent of students who showcased Oakwood to its national constituents.

It is clear from the records that he was invited to Oakwood in 1934 to "head" or "chair" the Bible Department; nevertheless, the thought has been advanced that real chairman leadership came a little later when student enrollment increased to the need of additional Bible teachers. Among the first to team up with him was William Webb whose instructional load included biblical Greek. Steady student growth, especially large numbers of World War II veterans bringing enrollment to six hundred, sparked Moseley to request of President Moran and the Board of Trustees even more teachers, namely: Clarence T. Richards and Ernest E. Rogers. Shortly after these two instructors were invited to the faculty, the little son of the Webb family was laid to rest; and the Webbs accepted a call to pastor in California. Rogers succeeded Webb as the teacher of Greek. Oakwood Junior College grew into Oakwood College by 1944-45 riding a momentum that sparked and inspired progress across the entire academic spectrum. Doubtless, with the arrival of a number of new faculty and staff, the most telling infusing of academic strength came with the arrival of Dr. Eva B. Dykes from Howard University wearing, with her various distinctions, the privilege of being the first African American female to complete the requirements for the Ph.D. degree. Her coming to the Oakwood campus was tantamount to a blood transfusion bringing new and confident life for the present and future of Christian education at the Huntsville school.

Undergirding the regular classes taught for ministerial majors, Moseley instituted the well-known Ministerial Seminar which brought students and staff together every Friday evening. Before formal classes were developed in Pastoral Ministry and Public Evangelism, the weekly Seminar would cover such areas through presentations and/or practical demonstrations like mock church board meetings, funerals, weddings, baptisms services and so on. Moseley himself brought to the table what he himself had experienced as a pastor and what he had learned from working with evangelists George E. Peters (most successful black evangelist at that time, 1930's) and Herbert Green. He also requested contemporary pastors and evangelists to prepare written procedures of their ministry and send them to the Religion Department with the understanding that his purpose was to share with students in training. For then and decades into the future, general knowledge asserted that up to 90% or more of black ministers in North America were graduates of the Oakwood program. If we were to begin calling personal names here of pastors, evangelists, church leaders and religious educators who were alumni of the religion and theology program by Elder Calvin E. Moseley, Jr., at Oakwood University, the scroll would be long and laudatory. Just to create some time boundary for personal research or inquiry on this point, should anyone be interested in documenting what might otherwise be anecdotal, start with the mid-1930's through 1951 when Moseley resigned from Oakwood. Develop the roster of names and tally the number of active African-American ministers of that era who were taught by the "Rabbi." You would then understand why the 90% estimate mentioned above is often quoted as more truth than imagination. (Would you desire to add more grist to the mill? Then consider also the students under his tutelage during his part-time teaching for another fifteen or so years when he returned to the Oakwood scene following his 1971 retirement from the General Conference.)

Perhaps no one has captured the profile of Moseley the teacher-preacher and Moseley the preacher-teacher better than one of his contemporaries, Louis B. Reynolds: "Calvin E. Moseley, Jr., who came to the campus as a Bible teacher in 1934, perhaps did the most to inspire and prepare young men for the ministry. An excellent preacher himself, it was only natural that students would imitate his style, lean heavily on his notes. Although Christian standards underwent frenzied upheaval during the l930's, Moseley stood solidly as a block of granite for the plain virtues. He was the disciplined student of guarded emotions and restrained impulses, for whom work and thrift formed a holy creed. He insisted on simple, unadorned dress for preachers and Bible instructors. Beyond the social niceties, Moseley believed, lay the deeper issue of responsibility, of example, in carrying the Advent message. 'After all, gentlemen,' he used to say, 'people tend to look more at you than at the Word you preach.' " *(We Have Tomorrow [The Story of American Seventh-day Adventists with an African Heritage],* Hagerstown: Review and Herald Publishing Association, 1984, p. 208) Listening to that distinct and prophetic note of their inspired teacher over the years, his students called him "Rabbi."

Increasing while Decreasing

Over a two or three year period of continued student enrollment growth at a time when he and Mrs. Moseley were expecting an addition to their family, Moseley was ecstatic when relieved of being dean of men which allowed him, wife and baby to move across campus into a faculty residence called "The Pines." There his family could enjoy improved living accommodations and prepare for the birth of their second daughter, Barbara, who would be the first baby delivered in the Riverside Sanitarium (Nashville, Tennessee) by Dr. T. R. M. Howard, an Oakwood and Loma Linda Medical School graduate. After her daughters Harriet Ann and Barbara enrolled in elementary school, Mrs. Moseley (a nursing graduate of Hinsdale Sanitarium in 1931) would spend more time as Oakwood nurse and teaching courses. Both daughters grew up to attend school on the Oakwood campus from elementary through academy and then years at Oakwood College. Some two decades later, late-1950's, following their father's seventeen years of teaching and pastoring at Oakwood, they joined their parents in Takoma Park, Maryland when their father transferred to the General Conference of Seventh-day Adventists. Initially, Harriet Ann and later her sister Barbara enrolled at Columbia Union College (now Washington Adventist University). Harriet happened to be the first African-American to racially integrate CUC. But for now, back to the "Oaks" lest we get ahead of ourselves in time.

One thing often noted about Moseley's developing and directing the ministerial program at Oakwood is that he had to structure the curriculum and pastoral training format from scratch without an existing blueprint. Girding up his mind and rolling up his sleeves with Bible in one hand and the writings of Ellen White in the other, his determination drenched itself in sincerity and conviction and structured a ministerial blueprint second to none and one which, inevitably, would bear the Moseley imprint all over it. When Oakwood became a senior college in 1945, an enrichment program was instituted that invited educators to come to the campus from various sister colleges in the North American Division and from the General Conference. George Vandeman, director of the highly successful telecast, "It Is Written," was assigned to visit and appraise the ministerial classes. Upon concluding his audit, Vandeman was asked by Moseley: "How do you evaluate the ministerial program at Oakwood in relationship to our sister colleges in North

America?" Vandeman looked at him, smiled and then replied: "There is no comparison. You have the best all-round program of any of the colleges I have visited." The proof of the pudding would show itself in producing ministerial excellence and some of the best preachers of the SDA denomination. When the first black conference was voted (Lake Region, July 17, 1944) and other regional conferences subsequently established, Oakwood-trained graduates filled many if not most of the positions needed for leadership. That trend continued into the twenty first century as the Oakwood minister remained central and crucial to the operation and success of regional conferences in advancing the gospel commission of Jesus Christ (Matthew 28:19-20).

The most recent report of the phenomenal growth of regional or black conferences reveals the following:

1945		2014	
Churches:	230	Churches:	1,174
Membership:	17,814	Membership:	300,825
Tithe:	$224,660.	Tithe:	$170,092,396.
Baptisms/Prof. of Faith	848	Baptisms/Prof of Faith	8,042
Mission Offering	$72,122.	Mission Offering	$2,331,022.
% of GC/NAD Tithe (No NAD in 1945)	6%	% of GC/NAD Tithe	18%
% of NAD Membership	8%	% of NAD Membership	25%
(Source: Regional Voice, Fall, 2015, p. 36. Published by the Office of Regional Affairs/www.regionalconferenceministry.com)			

The report goes on to say of the five financially largest SDA divisions around the world (from the North American Division to the South Pacific Division), the conglomerate financial strength of the nine Regional Conferences would rank them number 4 in the lineup, that is, if they were a division. The report further states that the "Top five divisions plus the Regional Conferences of NAD provide 90.5% of the total tithe income for the General Conference."

The point worth asserting here credits the graduates of the ministerial program by Elder Moseley at Oakwood for being the primary feeder of leaders, pastors, and evangelists to these successful conferences. That trend of providing up to 90% of pastors, evangelists, and other leaders for regional conferences continued appreciably over the decades. This is certainly not the place to try to call the roll of all the Moseley students who served and are serving valiantly in pastoral, evangelistic, and other areas of ministry and education. Prototypes of his students might be personified in at least three or four persons, namely: Charles E. Bradford (presidential leadership for local conference and North American Division; Earl E. Cleveland (local, union, and general conference evangelist); Charles D. Brooks (pastor and eminent broadcast preacher; GC Field Secretary); and Calvin B. Rock (university president, general conference vice-president, chairman of university boards). In recognition of the stellar contributions of the initial three persons above, Oakwood University erected on its campus the Bradford-Cleveland-Brooks Leadership Center – Harold Lee its first director.

To a lesser degree beginning with the post civil rights era, the percentage of ministers being educated at Oakwood began diminishing when students of color were more aggressively recruited by other SDA schools and when these students felt increasingly more comfortable and disposed toward racially integrated environs.

The following list of nine presidents of regional conferences at their *inception* in the NAD reflects the comprehensive Moseley-Oakwood influence although there is lack of sure documentation regarding two of them: J. G. Dascent (1946-1951); W. W. Fordham (1947-1954); H. R. Murphy (1946-1954); H. Singleton (1946-1953); Louis Bland (1946-1953); T. M. Rowe (1947-1948); W. Starks (1967-1968); W. A. Thompson (1967-1970); J. A Edgecombe (1981-1988). According to my count, by the year 2005, there had been a total of sixty-seven (67) regional presidents, fifty-seven (or 85%) of whom were prepared for ministry at Oakwood

University. The nine incumbents of 2005 included seven Oakwood alums. Names of all nine are: Trevor H. C. Baker (Northeastern Conference), Benjamin P. Browne (South Central Conference), G. Alex Bryant (Central States Conference), Charles Cheatham (Allegheny East Conference), Jerome Davis (Lake Region Conference), James Lewis (Central States Conference), Vanard Mendinghall (South Atlantic Conference), Willie Taylor (Southeastern Conference), Billy E. Wright (Southwest Region Conference).

The Oakwood tradition of feeding workers especially into regional conferences continues into the twenty-first century but with the anecdotal estimation that "most" (without an established percentage) of the ministers in those conferences are clearly Oakwood University alums. Of course, Oakwood (as all SDA colleges and universities) prepares its students to serve the world church without regard to ethnicity.

Profiles and Personality

Most portrayals of the man Calvin Moseley paint him as spiritual, thoughtful, congenial, and down to earth while at the same time straightforward, authoritative, and transparent. A person of deep conviction and measured words, he believed he owed it to you and his conscience to "speak the truth" as he saw it or not at all. Years later in the 1960's when he had moved on from Oakwood College to the General Conference and I had become his son-in-law and a teacher at Oakwood, I was strolling across the campus and happened to meet Ms. Eugenia I. Cunningham affectionately known to all as "Mother Cunningham" after whom Cunningham Hall was named. A saintly personality at "The Oaks" for half a century, she had known Moseley when he was a student, when he returned to chair the Religion Department, and when his second daughter, Barbara, was born. "Brother Warren," she said to me warmly and maternally, "how are you and my girl Barbara faring? How's married life? Tell me about your new work as a teacher.

How is everything?" My quick response was "Very, very well, Mrs. Cunningham. Things are par excellent and couldn't be better!" I can still hear her voice coming through her half but friendly smile when she then replied: "Well, I think I'll ask Barbara too. She'll tell me the whole truth. *She's a Moseley you know.*" I believe she thought my words were a bit "gilding the lily" while she preferred down to earth reality. At any rate, I clearly got her message implying that chips don't fall too far from the stump; and if she wanted to get an honest-to-goodness report, she would have to ask a Moseley. With that, she bid me "good day" and encouraged me to burn my bridges, a reference to my waves of sacrifices and challenges back in Dallas, Texas which I navigated to come to Oakwood ten years earlier when a student. Doubtless, she had learned about my Dallas background from her son Charles Cunningham, Youth Leader of Southwest Region Conference, who had personally driven me in his car to attend Oakwood as a freshman.

Moseley the straight shooter—that is precisely how his peers and protégés usually profiled him, one who spoke his mind in fair weather or foul. A general perception floated around that with Elder Moseley "everything was black or white with few, if any, grey areas." Most persons gave him high marks and compliments for his candidness and unvarnished veracity. Some avoided him when convenient. A few students and staff peers, it is alleged, had apparent personality clashes and philosophical differences with the Rabbi to the extent of chafing under his counsel they considered acerbic and at times thinking his advise danced very close to chastisement. Most student-teacher interaction took place in his Bible and homiletic classes the latter which entailed sermon and preaching evaluation. His typical evaluation and scrutiny of students during classroom sermon critiques sought to encourage and inspire but occasionally struck fear. An oft-repeated story over the years reports that the Rabbi told one of his students he would never make it in ministry. That same student became one of the most outstanding soul-winning preachers in the history of Adventism. Because that oft-repeated prediction went awry, some of the other students who had chafed a bit under the careful tutelage of the Rabbi took a modicum of comfort. However, that particular student who went from "rags" of the Rabbi's prediction to "riches" of a better outcome said to me personally one day that if he when a student had continued in the direction he was traveling when Moseley saw less in his future, he would indeed have fulfilled his teacher's negative "prophecy." Sharing this with me sounded very much like his endorsement and appreciation of the sound counsel that Rabbi Moseley was attempting to give. At any rate, his students tend to affirm unequivocally that the Rabbi taught with unfeigned love and unaffected sincerity and earned their unalloyed respect and esteem as one who had a pure heart.

Big Brother, Little Brother

The year of 1931 found older brother, Calvin, pastoring his first church in Evanston, Illinois, and younger brother, Ernest, continuing his education at Oakwood Junior College. While older brother was being highlighted as a bright prospect for church leadership, younger brother shared the brave spotlight of the 1931 student strike at Oakwood Junior College with other visionaries on behalf of quality and justice in areas of instruction, facilities, interpersonal relations between students and white faculty/staff and also between white faculty/staff and black teachers. The Oakwood Board voted that "Whereas the spirit of rebellion on the part of students must in no way be countenanced and meet our unqualified disapproval. We recommend that the leaders in the rebellion and persistent agitation at Oakwood Junior College during this year be dismissed at once by the faculty, and further, that they be not readmitted during the year 1932-1933." (Minutes, Board of Oakwood Junior College, May 10, 1932)

Student leaders identified as most responsible for the strike were the forcible five: Alan Anderson, Jr., Walter W. Fordham, Samuel Rashford, Herman R. Murphy, and Ernest Moseley, Calvin's brother. While most of these students weathered the storm in their own ways and continued their relation with both Oakwood and the Seventh-day Adventist Church throughout their futures, Ernest became disenchanted and remained outside the fellowship for some twenty years. Walter W. Fordham wrote an autobiography in 1990, fifty-nine years following the strike entitled *Righteous Rebel* where he states on page 34: "Ernest became discouraged after leaving Oakwood. He stumbled along the way, spiritually speaking, for a number of years. I had no contact with Ernest until many years later when I visited him in Los Angeles, California. How glad I was to see him, and he was overjoyed to see me. We spent hours together reminiscing over our experiences at Oakwood. Ernest died a few years later. I am sure he renewed his personal relationship with our merciful and loving Saviour."

I personally met him as "Uncle Ernest" also in Los Angeles (during the mid to late 1960's when I had married his niece, Barbara), and he introduced me to "Aunt Ethel," his wife. Actually, my being there was a faculty assignment of co-chaperoning with Dr. Gaines Partridge the traveling Aeolians from Oakwood University on a west coast concert tour. When we and our bus full of student singers arrived at the University Church in L. A., we were greeted warmly by Pastor Jonathan Allison and another ingratiating man with a familiar smile reminiscent of Calvin Moseley. I soon understood why the resemblance. I was looking at Ernest Moseley, my father-in-law's younger brother. He had not only returned to his church family (the spiritual community to which he had introduced his own father, mother, and brother back in Mississippi during the early 1920's) but was now immersing himself in lay church activities. He enthusiastically led out in placing our Oakwood students and staff into various homes for temporary lodging which appeared a joyous privilege to him! He had indeed made peace with His God and with his alma mater.

Expanding Pastures

In June of 1934, the Advanced Bible School was started by the General Conference of the SDA Church for Bible teachers whose first term Calvin Moseley attended on the campus of Pacific Union College in California. By 1937, the General Conference established the SDA Seminary in Takoma Park, Maryland (just outside the District of Columbia) where Moseley attended three additional terms. He earned the M.A. degree in religion from the seminary in 1944, having also written a thesis entitled: *Practices of Evangelism by Negro Methodists and Baptists Compared with Those of Negro Seventh-day Adventists*. At the time, the only published book out on evangelism in the Adventist church was by Elder J. L. Shuler, a caucasian minister. For the Moseley thesis research, his principal initial interviewee was Dr. Howard Thurman, Dean of the Divinity School of Howard University. Informed by Thurman that no literature existed by Negroes on black preachers doing evangelism, Moseley followed his suggestion to "talk to the men in the field, men who are out there doing it. Interview them each!"

Moseley drew up a questionnaire of things he wanted to know, had it approved by faculty at Emmanuel Missionary College, by faculty at the SDA Seminary, took a whole summer off and went to every major city east of the Mississippi River. He shared with the Oakwood University Archivist, Clara Peterson Rock: "I went to every one of them, and I spoke to every important man in evangelism that I could find and . . . on the assumption of course that the greatest churches, the larger churches and the greatest soul-winners were in those churches. So I went to every black Methodist and Baptist Church of any consequence in every major city from St. Louis to New York and from Chicago southward. I went to them all and talked with them personally and submitted my questions to them, got their answers, and that's the result of it." (Interview,

Archivist Department, Eva B. Dykes Library, Oakwood University, February 3, 1974)

Interestingly enough, following the resignation of President J. L. Moran in 1945, the same Oakwood College Board of Trustees, February 21, 1954, that received his abnegation voted to invite Calvin E. Moseley to the presidency. To the surprise of some but probably not to the surprise of many, he declined that opportunity to serve in the lead position of the institution. Without knowing the explicit reason for his declination, speculation surmises that the Rabbi knew he was at his best doing what he was always known to do: preach, teach, counsel, advise and, as well as he could, try to emulate the words of that Negro spiritual that his quartets and male choruses used to sing: "Lord, I want to be a Christian in my heart."

Fifteen-plus years of multitasking at Oakwood College since joining the faculty in 1934 began to drag on Moseley a bit and prompted him to seek a sabbatical for a change of pace and fresh venues. (Of course, attending his garden, a favorite hobby, brought him refreshment and special satisfaction when sharing the harvest with the Oakwood campus orphanage managed by Mrs. Lilage Eggleston at one time and Mr. and Mrs. A. Walter Kimbrough at another. Moseley has gone on record testifying that tithing his garden so blessed it that practically the entire faculty was invited to share the harvest). However, refreshment here and there notwithstanding, his inner soul desired some measure of reprieve from daily rounds of 1) chairing the Religion Department, 2) teaching classes (also periodically in the academy or high school), 3) pastoring the Oakwood College Church, 4) pastoring the First SDA Church in the Huntsville community, 5) directing and traveling with the male chorus (also Alabama Singers including female singers), 6) academic advising, 7) personal counseling, 8) presiding over the Oakwood College National Alumni Association and along the way 9) writing a book: *The Lord's Day*. The plot was steadily thickening and nudging him to think time and again like the apostle Peter, who said: "I'm going fishing." (John 21:3) Personal time with family (wife and two early teen daughters) or tending his pet dog (Chang) or goats or honey bees or garden was happening less frequently than desired.

Just about the time of a scheduled meeting with a conference representative who desired to follow up on a "feeler" for Moseley to consider an invitation to return to fulltime pastoring of a large church, the Rabbi came down with a serious chill and high temperature of one hundred and two degrees! He happen to be on a male chorus trip but instantly was put to bed and under the doctor's care who diagnosed him with a severe case of influenza. He had to abandon the current male chorus tour he was directing and assigned a student member to complete the itinerary. The conference representative, wondering whether Moseley was reneging on his promise to confer, came personally to his bedside but found him in no condition to make a decision about transitioning to a church pastorate. Moseley then made his way back to the Oakwood campus. During his illness and upon giving more thought and prayer to the matter, he was impressed not to accept the invitation. A few weeks afterwards, he received a call in 1951 to join the General Conference of Seventh-day Adventists as a General Field Secretary.

The official invitation to the General Conference staff finally arrived, yet the Rabbi found himself harboring reservations. For two weeks he carried the letter in his pocket. His hesitancy stemmed not from any doubt of the invitation coming from the Lord. Rather his concern centered around the social climate in which he would be working. A call from the secretary/director of the North American Colored Department of the GC, G. E. Peters, prodded his conscience to delay no longer. The message said: "Answer is needed by Autumn Council time." Consulting with his wife, Moseley asked her: "How do you feel about it?" She replied: "I don't want to go either." Both decided to pray about it and leave it in God's hands.

They returned to sleep, trusting Providence who had always guided their footsteps.

Upon awakening simultaneously, they looked at each other and smiled. "Still praying about it? How do you feel?" Moseley asked. Both were weighing the consequences an affirmative answer might have on the education of their two daughters. Beyond social concerns, there remained questions about financing their college tuition for which student employment on the Oakwood campus had covered the full year. Not sure that the move to the Columbia Union College (aka Washington Adventist University) area would provide such student work opportunity called for serious thought. Nevertheless, Moseley added: "I think we ought to try it." Mrs. Moseley echoed his response with "I do too." Happy that they both were Spirit-led to their personal decisions, nonetheless, they also decided like Gideon to "put out the fleece" once again. The Rabbi resolved that after attending the upcoming Autumn Council session in Washington, D. C., he would ask the General Conference president, W. H. Branson, if Mrs. Moseley and their daughters may remain at Oakwood for the remainder of the time covered by their earned tuition credit.

Hiccup or Stumbling Block?

While awaiting the Autumn Council and his transition to the General Conference location, Moseley was approached by President J. L. Moran of Oakwood to help him out of a jam. The school faced the risk of not meeting the scheduled time for completing a new campus building; therefore, Moran, very much acquainted with Moseley's master skill in plastering, apparently thought it appropriate to secure his help during this brief interim. Moseley agreed to assist under special arrangements. A Union Conference official happened to see him at work, felt it violated policy, and reported the matter to Moran. Moseley was not only ordered to cease and desist but also return all remuneration accrued. Even the General Conference was informed of the seeming conflict of interest by its newly appointed staff member. Moseley appealed to President Moran to inform the General Conference administration and the North American Division of the particulars, namely, that Moran himself initiated the request for Moseley's plastering work, that the premise for the request was an emergency in order to be ready for opening of school, and that the pay was only half the wage to the other plasters. The president of the North American Division, upon receiving the letter from Moran, responded immediately, telling Moseley of his appreciation for the contribution he had made to the college and expressing full confidence in his integrity. The incident was closed, and the Rabbi with joyful thanksgiving turned his attention to preparing for his new assignment in the world church.

A House Divided

Moseley reported to the 1951 Autumn Council session of the General Conference with mixed emotions, because the housing situation in the Takoma Park, Maryland–District of Columbia area was unresolved. His family was settled with living facilities on the campus of Oakwood College along with prepaid tuition for his daughters in tact. He now faced the task of finding comparable housing at his new location with financial questions tugging at him. To confer about such matters with the General Conference President, Elder W. H. Branson, during the Autumn Council sessions was virtually impossible. To his good fortune, however, Moseley was granted a fifteen minute audience, hardly sufficient time for a presentation of his needs and various things on his heart which needed immediate attention.

Frustration was knocking hard at the door of Moseley's heart, because rooms or apartments for rent to accommodate him and family were difficult to find. Racial discrimination did not make matters any easier. Elder G. E. Peters (director of the General

Conference Colored Department with whom Moseley was to serve as his associate) lent a hand to find living accommodations but without success. The appointment with President Branson being now only about ten minutes away, Peters continually underscored the urgency of being on time for the sake of respect to the president and in view of the crunch of others seeking his presence. All these pressures placed Moseley in a crossfire of temporary confusion. Steadying him during these anxious moments was the remembrance that he and Mrs. Moseley had prayed earnestly for God to resolve the situation to His glory.

Although Moseley was in the thick of room and apartment hunting, he decided to keep the appointment with President Branson. During the conversation when Moseley was explaining his lodging situation, almost without a beat Branson chimed in and asked him: "How would it be for your wife and children to remain at the college this year, and in the meantime you can be looking for accommodations?" Moseley responded gladly and with deep relief: "You have answered my prayer. I know the Lord put those words in your heart." God had once again given him full assurance of His guidance. The message reached his family with inestimable joy.

Transitions

After Moseley had spent two years at the General Conference as assistant director of the Regional Department and editor of the *Regional Informant* periodical, Elder George E. Peters, the director, became seriously ill and found it necessary to retire from active service. His retirement directly affected two areas of the regional structure of the church in the North American Division, namely: The Regional Department [formerly called the Colored Department] of the General Conference and the Oakwood College administration. Elder Frank L. Peterson, President of Oakwood College, received a call to fill the vacancy created by the retirement of George E. Peters. Simultaneously, Peterson was asked to remain as the Oakwood president until the next General Conference session, which would convene soon. Meanwhile, the GC asked Moseley to remain in the Regional Department to carry on its ministry until Elder Peterson arrived to take over his duties as director. Then Moseley would assume his new position of Field Secretary of the General Conference. It is quite appropriate here to list the names of all the predecessors of G. E. Peters in the Regional Department: J. W. Christian, A. J. Haysmer, C. B. Stephenson, and W. H. Green (first African-American to head this department). Peters succeeded Green and was followed immediately by Calvin E. Moseley and Frank L. Peterson.

During the interim of waiting for the upcoming General Conference convention, the Oakwood College Board and General Conference turned their thoughts toward finding a replacement for Peterson at the Oakwood presidency and looked to Moseley as recorded in the February 21, 1954 minutes of the Oakwood College Board. When the General Conference asked Moseley to accept the leadership at Oakwood as its president, he responded: "Brethren, I have served here in the General Conference for two years. I have not been to the university [more graduate education] for further study. What could I offer to the college that I have not already given? What some of you may or may not know, I have served in that capacity. When the president [James L. Moran] had to be away for an extended time for any cause, I was asked to sit for him. This occurred during at least half of my stay at the college. Summer after summer I have served as acting president. During those summers, I became convinced that this was not the vocation to which I wished to devote my life. For these two reasons I feel I must decline." (Walter M. Starks document, Archives of the Eva B. Dykes Library of Oakwood University) He since, however, touched the leadership of the ensuing nine Oakwood presidents to the present Dr. Leslie N. Pollard.

At the coming General Conference session, Elder Frank L.

Peterson returned to General Conference service as the director of the Regional Department. Elder Moseley transitioned to a field secretary for the General Conference which included assisting Peterson in any way needed for the colored or regional work. In essence, the arrangement amounted to a joint appointment.

"Cleve" Joins His Teacher "Mose"

By the mid-1950's, the extraordinary soul-winning ministry of Elder Earl E. Cleveland soared to evangelistic heights previously unknown in the regional work of North America. His exploits began in the South Atlantic Conference headquartered in Atlanta. When he later served as the Southern Union evangelist, that particular Union enjoyed upwards of seven or eight hundred baptisms yearly resulting mainly from the personal baptisms by Cleveland himself and other pastor-evangelists whom he was inspiring and training. (Read details in his biography: *E. E. Cleveland [Evangelist Extraordinary]* by Harold Lee with Monte Sahlin published by Center for Creative Ministry, 2006).

Elder Moseley shared information and reports about the phenomenal soul-winning success of Cleveland with the president of the General Conference, Elder William H. Branson. He had wanted to know the reason for the membership growth of Southern Union. Moseley indentified the young evangelist Cleveland as the principal reason. Branson then inquired how could that young minister help other conferences to which Moseley said: "That's exactly why I brought this to you. We have tried to get the Southern Union to loan Cleveland to other conferences, but they will not cooperate." Then Branson suggested: "Well, can't we bring him to the General Conference, and let him serve out of here?" Moseley answered: "That might be the only way you can get it done to use him in other conferences." Elder Branson proceeded to encourage that Moseley take the lead in the matter by asserting: "If you can sell this to these other folks as you have sold it to me, we'll get brother Cleveland." He then commissioned Moseley to approach the union presidents in the North American Division the itinerary for which Branson himself arranged. Moseley visited all the union presidents and, in his own words: "Under God I was able to convince them as I had convinced him that Cleveland was needed to be used in North America to train young evangelists in the field . . . service training." (Walter M. Starks document, Archives of Eva B. Dykes Library of Oakwood University)

Before Elder Cleveland came to the notice of the GC president, I remember his coming to the Oakwood University campus yearly to conduct a week's evangelistic workshop for us students in the early 1950's. As a matter of fact, his soul-winning campaign in the city of Montgomery, Alabama, was conducted in 1954 under a tent on the corner of Smythe and High Streets. His evangelistic team included the Collegiate Quartet (James Edgecombe, Benjamin Reaves, William Scales, and Elbert Shepperd, all Oakwood students). I tagged along and was utilized by Elder Cleveland especially to recite religious poetry usually during Sabbath afternoon programs under the "Canvas Cathedral." This Montgomery, Alabama, evangelism happened to be also the time when he was visited by a young pastor named Dr. Martin Luther King, Jr. who was in the early months of his initial pastorate at the Dexter Avenue Baptist Church. King and his ministerial companion, Pastor Ralph D. Abernathy as I recall, wanted to meet the dynamic Adventist preacher Cleveland and appeal for peace and harmony among the local churches considering that so many members of the Sunday churches were being attracted to, convicted by, and baptized into Jesus Christ in the context of the Three Angels' Messages.

Another occurrence regarding the Montgomery meeting was told to me in retrospect by Cleveland himself. An "observation visit" by Elder R. Allan Anderson of the General Conference was paid to Montgomery, Alabama, and the evangelistic site incognito to witness with his own eyes the young phenomenal evangelist in action. No doubt it had already been determined that should Cleveland be invited to the General Conference staff, he would be placed in the Ministerial Department of which Anderson was director. At some point in 1954, the official invitation was extended, and Cleveland accepted. Elder Branson, however, was soon succeeded by the new president of the General Conference, Elder R. R. Figuhr, who had other ideas. Rather than utilizing Cleveland to grow regional conferences in North America according to the original idea, Figuhr had heard of his anointed exploits and forthwith decided that he wanted him available for the world field. After some persuasion along the way, the "world field" comprised not merely Africa, Europe, and the Caribbean but also large city evangelism in black communities like Detroit, Chicago, New York, Los Angeles, Oakland, New Orleans.

While I was a student in the SDA Seminary in Takoma Park, before having to follow the campus relocation to Berrien Springs, Michigan, I found joy and inspiration visiting the General Conference Offices of Elder Frank L. Peterson, Elder Calvin E. Moseley, and Elder E. E. Cleveland who were the only African American leaders there. Cleveland gets the gold star for being the first Oakwood student of Moseley to join the General Conference staff. In years following through 2015, others taught or influenced by Moseley and having served in the GC are (alphabetically): Delbert Baker (Vice Pres.), Warren Banfield (Regional Dept), Rosa Banks (Secretariat), Richard Barron (Youth), Russell Bates (Lay Activities), Maurice Battle (Secretariat), Alex Bryant (NAD Sec.), Charles Bradford (NAD President/GC), Charles Brooks (Field Sec.), Walter Fordham (Regional Dept.), Murray Joiner (Personal Ministry), Frank Jones (Treasury), Dennis Keith (Treasury), Samuel Myers (Stewardship), Walter Pearson (Ministerial), Wintley Phipps (Religion Lib/. . . Congress), Calvin Rock (Vice Pres.), Walter Starks (Stewardship), Meade Van Putten (Treasury), DeWitt Williams (Health and Medical), Robert Woodfork (Ministerial) and

Henry Wright (Ministerial). What a valiant group! I move they be inducted into the "Moseley 'Students-in-the-GC' Hall of Fame." No second necessary. Incumbent GC president and spiritual leader, 2017, is Ted N. C. Wilson. Daniel R. Jackson currently serves the North American Division as president.

Full Steam Ahead: at Home and Abroad

Elder and Mrs. Moseley finally moved to Takoma Park, Maryland—the location of both the General Conference Office and Columbia Union College [aka Washington Adventist University]. Both daughters, Harriet Ann and Barbara Jean, remained at Oakwood, the former in college and the latter in academy or high school. During a time in the academy, Barbara and her friend, Althea Lee, both lived in the home of Elder Frank and Mrs. Bessie Peterson, president and first lady of the college. Later Barbara joined her sister in the Oakwood dorm, Cunningham Hall. By 1955, Harriet Ann transferred to Columbia Union College as the first African-American to integrate that institution and graduate there (1956). Barbara transferred from Oakwood University and enrolled at CUC/WAU in 1957 and graduated by 1959.

Her graduation brought us to the magic moment she and I waited for to fulfill the agreement with her father for marriage. She was now a college graduate and I a seminary student. We wasted no time: her graduation on June 6, 1959 and our wedding on June 14, 1959. Location: First Seventh-day Adventist Church on 8th and Shepherd, NW, in Washington, D.C. We resided in seminary housing for African-Americans on Colby Street just off Sligo Creek Avenue in Takoma Park. I completed my Master's Degree that same year in Homiletics and Speech at the SDA Seminary and then by 1961 finished the erstwhile Bachelor of Divinity (B.D. degree which the Association of Theological Schools changed to Master of Divinity [M. Div.]). After contemplating whether to accept the privilege of a pastorate in a certain northern city or the privilege of teaching religion at Oakwood University, I believed that God wanted me join the Oakwood faculty.

From another perspective, my decision to teach at Oakwood really meant *déjà vu* for my wife, Barbara, who was going back to where she was born and had spent most of her life. She remembered her early years in Oakwood kindergarten, elementary school, academy, and university where she studied through her sophomore year. Having transferred from Oakwood to study only two years at CUC, her backtracking to Oakwood was not unlike the Nicodemus question in John 3:4 of returning to his mother's womb to be born again. More than once I had to field the question from our friends: "Now how fair was that? Could you not have waited until she got to see other parts of the world before returning to the cotton fields of Alabama?" Furthermore, allowing myself to become even more vulnerable, our maiden year of teaching at Oakwood in 1961 stretched to over half a century. Barbara did get a breather from the rarified air of Oakwood when we spent about three years for my doctoral studies at Michigan State University and pastoring in the Lake Region Conference (Benton Harbor-Niles-Dowagiac, Michigan) where I was ordained to the gospel ministry during the presidency of Elder Charles E. Bradford. All of our three children (Mervyn, Karis, and Shana) were born on the Oakwood campus, attended and graduated from elementary, academy, and Oakwood University (except for Karis who did a senior year at Pine Forge Academy plus graduation). Son Eugene Warren and granddaughter Shelli Warren were born in Texas and Nebraska respectively. Daughter Karis Warren's family includes sons: Malachiae Warren and Michael Dobson, Jr. and daughter: Imani Dobson. Daughter Shana Byers' family includes husband: Timothy and daughters: Ashlee, Asia, Autumn and Ayana. Beginning with Merv, all through the bloodline of Calvin Edwin Moseley, Jr.

Of course, Barbara herself has not been idle professionally speaking. Attaining her Master's Degree in Early Childhood Education at A&M University, she served on the Oakwood faculty for thirty years. Her sister, Harriet Ann, worked for years in the public sector in Minnesota, and Harriet's husband, Donald Keith, spent decades in the health profession as a nurse anesthetist. Their daughters, Lori and Karmen, both attended Oakwood University where Lori graduated. Lori is married to Larry Fullard, and they have two sons, Larry, Jr. and Lamar. Thus you have a brief profile of the immediate family of Calvin E. Moseley, Jr. and wife Harriet Frances (Slater) Moseley. It is appropriate here to catch up on the family of Ernest Moseley, Calvin's younger brother who led his parents and older brother Calvin to the evangelistic meeting that changed the trajectory of their lives. The family of uncle Ernest grew up and lived mostly in California. Their names are: Augusta (mother of his children); Sons: Eddie and Ernest, Jr.; Daughters: Frances and Lillie Belle; Ethel (second wife).

Now back at the ranch so to speak, the General Conference Office. Elder Moseley was accustomed to being a very popular preacher for church revivals and camp meetings. He looked forward to those types of engagements shaping a slice of his GC calendar. But what a surprise upon his arrival in 1951! Right away his routine bespeaking for God would instantly take on a more global dimension. George E. Peters, his associate in the Regional Department, was scheduled to go to West Africa for the special assignment of developing the overseas program—a first for an African American. Prior to leaving, his medical exam discovered a heart condition which prevented him from making that trip. Understandably, he would ask his co-worker to stand in the gap and go instead. Only three days later, after having just arrived at the General Conference, Moseley found himself on a plane to West Africa. His assignment included learning about their country, developing their church programs, teaching, preaching, inspiring, organizing, and evangelizing.

How refreshing to meet up in West Africa with several other

African Americans whom he knew were already serving as missionaries there! Most of them he had taught back at Oakwood. His mission proved even more a pleasure working there with Dunbar Henri (Lorraine), Maurice Battle (Esther), Phillip Giddings (Violet), Lucius Daniel (Naomi) and Leland Mitchell (Lottie). Africa became the first of five continents he would serve during his two decades of General Conference tenure.

The Holy Spirit used Moseley in West Africa to baptize 1,509 souls into a saving relationship with Jesus Christ. Another country of extended stay for him was Egypt (especially Cairo) where he spent eleven weeks preaching, teaching, and evangelizing. Materials on file in the Oakwood University Archives point to his revolutionizing the whole work of Seventh-day Adventism in the Middle East at the time. Whereas the entire Middle East Division of Moslems was known for eight to ten or maybe fifteen baptisms yearly, the Lord blessed one Moseley evangelistic meeting alone to yield thirteen baptisms plus seventy-five persons taking part in preparation for baptism at the time of his leaving. I remember Mrs. Moseley accompanying him on his assignment to Poland where they were very warmly received and appreciated for their ministry. As a General Conference representative, he logged some serious air miles travelling to every continent except Australia and South Africa. I personally recall churches in the U.S. looking forward expectantly to see the photographs and video "slides" of his work and travels to foreign fields. These were special treats which churches anticipated from all missionaries. On one occasion, Moseley shocked and saddened the expectant audience when reporting his luggage being stolen in a certain European city while he and another missionary from America (I think it was Maurice Battle) were traveling together. Lost luggage is one thing, but lost luggage containing your sermons can send a preacher into a tailspin of despondency. When you consider that his sermons were handwritten with no computer backup or "hard drive," you can feel the depth of his loss.

Furthermore, those sermon manuscripts were carried with him overseas for endless appointments and occasions (worship, evangelism, workers' meetings, educational assemblies and so on). He certainly deserved the right to experience painful disappointment which I know he did. After a while when cloudy skies of remorse gradually thinned somewhat, I heard him remark in typical pungent serio-comic Moseley style: "Whoever that bird was who got my sermons, I hope he reads himself into the Kingdom of Jesus Christ." Not a bad thought. Who knows? If books, articles, tracts, and the internet can bespeak for God, why not stolen sermons? Especially if they belong to the Rabbi!

When back in the U. S. itself, Moseley faced a galaxy of requests especially for his preaching. Revivals and camp meetings rose to the top of his appointment schedule. From the mid 1950's and the emergence of the civil rights movement (ala the bus boycott in Montgomery, Alabama, 1955) to the March on Washington (1963) and the assassination of Dr. Martin Luther King, Jr. (1968), the General Conference ministry of Moseley reached the apex of its heyday. These were tense times both without and within the Seventh-day Adventist Church. At the heart of most discussions (if not debates, among SDA religious leaders) centered the notion of whether it was appropriate for Christians to engage in what many defined a socio-political movement. Adventist ministers and laity who considered the movement consistent with Christian theology and justice encouraged engagement and themselves participated in civil/human rights endeavors across the face of the nation. Washington, D. C. found a significant presence of Adventists some participating both on a personal basis and others officially representing the SDA church particularly for 1) The March on Washington when Dr. King delivered his enduring "I Have a Dream" speech; and 2) The Resurrection City campaign for the poor symbolized by six muddy weeks of tent dwelling by 3,000 persons on the National Mall, beginning May 12, 1968. Regarding his official conversations with General Conference leaders, Moseley had been heard in their circles to characterize the conservative wing as "dealing in skins" (his words) rather than understanding the human rights movement to be a mandate to "Love the Lord your God with all your heart and with all your soul and with all your mind . . . and love your neighbor as yourself." (Matthew 22:37-39) Admittedly, Moseley expressed in other settings his personal challenge of trying to relate to some of the external codes of black experience like huge afro hair styles and uncensored music trends which he believed were clashing with the traditional and great church music of hymns, anthems, classics, and Negro spirituals. The spirit of self-determination for African Americans fed by the civil-human rights momentum revealed itself also among the regional conference leadership initiating serious talks in 1968 through about 1981 for black union conferences in the North American Division. So far, thoughts and expressions by Moseley himself on black unions are not among his archival materials. It may be that because the dawn of the black union dialogue (1968) came so near his twilight years of General Conference service and eventual retirement (1971), he was more into unloading his leadership luggage than repacking for another round of extensive polemics. Otherwise, as do others who knew him, I believe the Rabbi would certainly have had a point of view to share.

God and Goals

We shall ever in this life try to catch that special lightning in a bottle that explains the sure road and meaning of success. Explanations abound. I did read about one success formula which I would adapt to apply to Calvin Edwin Moseley, Jr.

1. He engaged himself in what he fully enjoyed (family, ministry, music, gardening, apiculture, fishing, and animals).
2. He never expected or asked for something for nothing.

3. He gave more than he got.
4. He was never satisfied with the status quo.
5. He did not feel sorry for himself.
6. He knew his abilities and his limitations.
7. He loved the Lord his God with all his heart, soul, and mind and loved his neighbors, students, parishioners, fellow workers, family and friends as himself (Matthew 22:37-39).

r
a
b
b
I N T E R M I T T I N G

Twenty years of General Conference service, 1951-1971. Calvin Edwin Moseley, Jr. could savor a clear conscience for having faithfully engaged himself in the work of God. His world church agenda covered a healthy variety of assignments: a) national and international gatherings; b) preaching; c) counseling; d) camp meetings; e) worship services; f) evangelistic efforts; g) committee sessions; h) boards (including Oakwood University and Riverside Sanitarium); i) advising; j) problem-solving; k) a monthly feature for *Message Magazine* called "Bible Answers to Your Questions;" l) editing *The Informant*, the news and reporting journal by the Regional Department of the General Conference and forerunner of the modern *Regional Voice* by regional conferences; and m) articles for the *Advent Review, Youth's Instructor, Signs of the Times, Message Magazine, These Times*. Two decades of productive service blessed him immeasurably as well as those to whom he ministered. However, over time, wear and tear took their toll, and Moseley decided to walk through the door of retirement. I felt his weariness one day when he told me that he increasingly knew that signals to shift gears were clearly flashing. He was pretty graphic in describing days when he would reach the point of going to work at the General Conference facility in Takoma Park, Maryland, and the moment he "set foot on the first step of the building" a feeling of something just short of dread would come over him. Translation? Change of pace and new scenery were screaming for his attention. His heart appealed for transition, for suspending and intermitting present grooves, and creating new ones.

Would he remain in the Maryland area where he and Mrs. Moseley were such happy citizens? How about sunny Florida where he loved to visit with a minister friend of his, Elder Edgar Lockett, who took him fishing whenever Moseley got a chance to visit the area? It is no surprise that the Moseley minds seriously turned to Alabama. In a real sense, Moseley roots were deeper there than anywhere else, and for that reason alone Alabama plus Oakwood University as a package faced few if any real competitors. So before the ink had scarcely dried on his official GC retirement papers, Elder and Mrs. Moseley headed for the red clay and cotton fields of his homeland. When he left Oakwood twenty years earlier, he carried the school with him in his heart, and now his heart returns him to Oakwood—not as staff or faculty but as a community resident available for whatever.

His return generated a mixture of excitement and curiosity. For not a few persons, a real face would finally be placed on a legendary figure they only heard of from time to time on campus. Especially three entities on the Oakwood landscape kept his name on our lips: The Moseley Complex building that houses the School of Religion; the foyer of the Oakwood University Church that hangs his portrait on the wall as its first African American pastor beginning 1934; and the Moseley-Warren Scholarship for religion and theology majors of Oakwood University. But now, 1972, some twenty years since his residing in the area, a "greater than a building or portrait or scholarship was here." The Rabbi himself in the flesh had returned. The campus pastor of the Oakwood campus church, Elder Eric C. Ward, wasted no time installing "Rabbi Moseley" as his First Elder. Oakwood University itself proceeded in a similar vein and contracted Moseley to teach part-time.

It goes without saying that after a twenty-year hiatus since experiencing daily interaction with youthful students on a day-to-day basis, Moseley himself and others wondered how he would fare with contemporary scholars accustomed to a more liberal give-and-take atmosphere in class and on campus. Would he be sufficiently comfortable and could he adjust to trends of free thought and honest disagreement reputedly so different from the academic milieu two decades earlier? When the prospect of the return of Moseley to his academic nest became a conversation item, I recall someone expressing to me the hope that the Rabbi be able to weather the culture shock which not a few said was awaiting him. I think we all were prayerfully anxious for him to make his best contribution to the modern generation. If others of us had been treading too far on the liberal edges of sacred boundaries, maybe Rabbi Moseley could assist in finding our way to a workable median without slipping to the opposite extreme. I suppose the basic question rearing its head was whether the colors black and white on certain issues of life would allow for at least a tinge of gray.

Fast forwarding to twenty years on this side of his retirement experience on the Oakwood University scene, he taught religion and preaching from 1973-90, served as Head Elder for the Oakwood University Church from 1974-94, and voted Alumnus of the Year at Alumni Homecoming in 1975. During those same years, my own tenure at Oakwood included chairing the Religion Department at the time Elder Moseley returned from the General Conference. From there, I served in several administrative areas of the university. President Calvin B. Rock, former ministerial student under Moseley, was the administrator who reached out to invite the Rabbi to the Oakwood community and classroom for his knowledge of Bible and preaching, his rich and broad experience of national and international service, and his impeccable ethos.

As an aside, Calvin B. Rock is the first and only person to serve in the OU presidency (1971-85) as a successor (though not immediate) to his own father-in-law, Frank L. Peterson, who also held that same position (1945-54). Similarly, I was granted the privilege to provide leadership as Chairman or Dean of the School Religion at Oakwood (1967-76; 1986-98; 2011-14), the same former position of my father-in-law, Calvin E. Moseley, Jr. (1934-51). For both Calvin Rock and me to follow our fathers-in-law in their identical leadership positions at Oakwood University certainly is unique. Other than that, I do not claim to know what this means except that history is history. Nevertheless, we all manifested shades of difference in our personalities and styles of delivering Christian education. Once again, we rely on Louis B. Reynolds for his summary profile of the Rabbi: "Calvin E. Moseley, Jr., who came to the campus as a Bible teacher in 1934, perhaps did the most to inspire and prepare young men for the ministry. An excellent preacher himself, it was only natural that students would imitate his style, lean heavily on his notes. Although Christian standards underwent frenzied upheaval during the 1930's, Moseley stood solidly as a block of granite for the plain virtues. He was the disciplined student of guarded emotions and restrained impulses, for whom work and thrift formed a holy creed. He insisted on simple, unadorned dress for preachers and Bible instructors. Beyond the social niceties, Moseley believed, lay the deeper issue of responsibility, of example, in carrying the Advent message. 'After all, gentlemen,' he used to say, 'people tend to look more at you than at the Word you preach.' " (Louis B. Reynolds, *We Have Tomorrow/The Story of American Seventh-day Adventists* with *an African Heritage.* Hagerstown: Review and Herald Publishing Association, 1984, 208).

The return of Moseley to the Oakwood campus proved a blessing to the institution and to himself. Students could witness with their own eyes the legendary personage they had only heard of before. But now in the classroom, in his "real clover," the Rabbi their pastors and parents talked about so endearingly could be seen, heard, and known for themselves. They would see a Bible teacher actually shed a tear, a male teacher at that, when he would translate a Biblical character into the first person, thus becoming that character for the here and now. Overcome by emotions when sensing the Bible character's heartthrob for sinners, Moseley himself became "the weeping prophet." (Lamentations 1:16) Such passion and pathos followed him also into the pulpit where contemporaries beheld a most unique personality declaring a unique gospel of a unique Savior in Jesus Christ!

Seventeen years (1934-1951), Calvin Edwin Moseley, Jr. chairs the religion department of Oakwood University presently chaired by Dr. Dedrick Blue. Twenty years (1951-1971), he serves in the General Conference of Seventh-day Adventists before retirement. Seventeen additional years after retirement and returning to Huntsville, Alabama (1973-1990), he once again teaches Bible in the Religion Department and also directs several male chorus groups. For twenty years (1974-1994) as a retiree, he also ministers as Head Elder under a staunch admirer Elder Eric C. Ward (Senior Pastor) of the Oakwood University Church presently shepherded in 2017 by Dr. Carlton P. Byrd the fourteenth pastor. Just think: Moseley serving seventeen years as Religion Chairman and Oakwood Church pastor (1934-1951), twenty years as a General Conference leader (1951-71), and then another twenty plus years (1973-1994) he teaches Bible and preaching while also ministering as Head Elder of the Oakwood University Church. What manner of man was this?

> "When God wants to drill a man
> And thrill a man and skill a man;
> When God wants to mold a man
> To play the noble's part;
> When He yearns with all His heart
> To create so great and bold a man
> That all the world shall praise—
> Watch His method watch His ways!
> How He ruthlessly perfects
> Whom He royally elects;

"How He hammers him and hurts him
And with mighty blows converts him
Into trial shapes of clay which
Only God can understand—
How He uses whom He chooses
And with every purpose fuses him,
By every art induces him
To try his splendor out—
Yes, God knows what He's about . . . ."
    —Anonymous

Calvin Edwin Moseley, Jr. The Rabbi. Created to succeed, designed to win, equipped to overcome, anointed to prosper, and blessed to become a blessing to his generation and through them to all generations to come.

CHRONOLOGY

Life and Service of Elder Calvin Edwin Moseley, Jr.

1906   On January 7, Calvin Edwin Moseley, Jr. is born to Calvin Edwin Moseley, Jr and Lilly Belle (Dixon) in Demopolis, Alabama.

1921   Completes three years of high school in Demopolis, Alabama.

1921   Attends Tuskegee Institute at age fifteen where he was appointed student messenger for President Robert Moton, successor to President Booker T. Washington, and where he was a member of a Bible class taught by the famous scientist, Dr. George Washington Carver.

1922   Moseley parents and brother Ernest are baptized into the Seventh-day Adventist Church by Elder F. S. Keitts after hearing Elders J. H. Laurence and Elder F. L. Peterson preach in an evangelistic tent meeting in Jackson, Mississippi but who turned the meetings over to Keitts to continue the services.

1923   Calvin Moseley, Jr. is baptized by Elder F. S. Keitts.

1923   Leaves Tuskegee and transfers to Jackson College in Jackson, Mississippi.

1925   Enrolls at Oakwood Junior College to study ministry and also becomes a member of the **Oakwood Jubilee Singers** (with Frank L. Peterson, John Wagner, Sr., and

Charles Salisbury) and the **Oakwood Nightingales** (same male singers but including females: Julia Baugh, Jennie Stratton, Viola Taylor, and Alga Bailey).

1927   Graduates from Oakwood Junior College.

1927   Enrolls in Emmanuel Missionary College (aka Andrews University).

1929   Graduates from Emmanuel Missionary College with a B. A. degree in Religion and History.

1929-30   Begins his first fulltime pastorate in Evanston, Illinois (including work in Springfield, Illinois).

1931-34   Continues his pastoral experience in St. Louis, Missouri.

1933   Marries Harriet Frances Slater in Shiloh SDA Church in Chicago, Illinois, June 15.

1934   Joins the Oakwood Junior College as Chairman of the Religion Department and Pastor of the Oakwood College Church (first African-American in both positions), the beginning of a seventeen (17) stint through 1951 of preparing believably 98 percent of the African American ministry for the Seventh-day Adventist Church.

1934   Attends the Advanced Bible School by General Conference of Seventh-day Adventists for Bible Teachers. Conducted on the campus of Pacific Union College in California.

1939-46   Serves as President of Oakwood Alumni Association.

1944   Earns the M. A. degree in Religion from the SDA Seminary in Takoma Park, Maryland. Thesis: *Practices of Evangelism by Negro Methodists and Baptists Compared with Those of Negro Seventh-day Adventists.*

1945-75 Approximate dates for writing monthly feature "Bible Answers to Your Questions," *The Message Magazine*, Southern Publishing Association. (Present *Message* editor, since 2012, Carmela Monk Crawford, is a successor to her father, Paul Monk, who edited same journal from 1980-85)

1949 Authors the book: *The Lord's Day,* Nashville*:* Southern Publishing Association.

1951 Senior ministerial students at Oakwood University construct and dedicate the campus Bell Tower to their beloved teacher, Elder Moseley.

1951-72 Joins the General Conference of SDA as Assistant Director of the Negro (later "Regional") Department and later Field Secretary for approximately two decades and travels to every continent except Australia and South Africa.

1951-72 Serves on the Board of Trustees of Oakwood College.

1951-72 Serves on the Board of Trustees of the Riverside Sanitarium in Nashville, Tenn.

1953-72 Serves as Editor of *The North American Informant,* periodical for the GC Regional Department. (Generally considered by many to be the forerunner of the current *Regional Voice Magazine* published by the Office of Regional Affairs)

1959   Performs the wedding ceremony (with Pastor Paul Cantrell) for his younger daughter, Barbara, to Mervyn A. Warren in First SDA Church in Washington, DC.

1961   Gives the hand of his older daughter, Harriet Ann, in marriage to Donald L. Keith on August 27. The wedding ceremony was performed in First Church of SDA in Washington, DC by the bride's uncle, Elder Fred B. Slater and the pastor, Elder Paul Cantrell.

1970   Receives an honorary LLD degree from Daniel Payne College in Birmingham, AL.

1971   Retires from the General Conference of SDA and thereafter sets up residence in Huntsville, Alabama.

1973   Begins an additional 17-year stint of teaching in the Religion Department which stretched to 1990.

1973   Authors the book: *Information Please/Bible Answers to Your Questions*, Washington, DC: Review and Herald Publishing Association, a compilation of materials from his *Message Magazine* feature: "Bible Answers to Your Questions," which he had been writing since the 1940's.

1974   Serves as Head Elder under Elder Eric C. Ward, Senior Pastor of the Oakwood University Church, a position he held for twenty years to 1994.

1976   The Oakwood Alumni Association honors him as Alumnus of the Year.

1977   Board of Trustees of Oakwood University names the

new Religion Building adjacent to the OU Church: The Moseley Complex.

1975 Approximate date for establishing an academic scholarship for religion and theology students known as the "C. E. Moseley Scholarship" later renamed the "Moseley-Warren Scholarship" reflecting the service of both Calvin E. Moseley, Jr. and his son-in-law, Mervyn A. Warren, alumni and faculty of the Religion Department at Oakwood University. (First created as a "loan" fund for seniors needing financial aid to graduate, it was later changed to a "merit" scholarship)

1983 Celebrates fifty years of marriage (June 15, 1933-June 15, 1983) to Harriet Frances Slater Moseley in a Reaffirmation Ceremony at the Oakwood University Church, Elder Calvin E. Ward, Senior Pastor.

1993 Celebrates sixtieth wedding anniversary.

1996 The Oakwood University Church (Leslie N. Pollard, Pastor) and the Archives Department of Eva B. Dykes Library of Oakwood University (Minneola Williams Dixon, Archivist) collaborate to create a "Heritage Wall of Calvin E. Moseley, Jr." in the church facility.

2000 C. E. Moseley and Mervyn Warren families establish the "Warren-Moseley Scholarship for Music Students" reflecting the choral, instrumental, and other musical contributions of both Elder Moseley and his grandson, Mervyn Edwin Warren, both alumni of Oakwood University and the latter also a graduate of the Department of Music.

2001   Concludes his life and labor of ninety-five years (January 7, 1906-January 28, 2001).

2001   Laid to rest in the Oakwood Memorial Gardens (February 5), the first to be buried there.

Lighthearted Looks
Along the Landscape

What would we do without the release of God-given laughter? The human journey of give and take, push and pull, ups and downs, success and failure finds cushion and soft landings in innocent parody. You soon discover that humor "is an attitude, one that takes life seriously but not too seriously. It is a matter of smiles, of laughter at times, and . . . a sincere reaching from person to person." ("Putting Humor to Work," *Washington Post/Health*, August 25, 1987.) The life and times of Calvin E. Moseley, Jr. was not without its moments of humor that evoked smiles and laughter evolving out of natural situations involving him. Here are a few recollections from his students and colleagues.

Miles of Smiles

Two cars. Two chaperones. One male chorus. Not enough snacks. What do you do when one car of student singers is "eating and drinking" while the other is practically "fasting"? It was customary that before departing from the Oakwood campus for the annual spring recruitment tour, delicious sack lunches are prepared to begin the journey. But among eager and youthful male singers, sack lunches are short-lived and destinations like Carolinas and New York are far ahead. Swifter than mockingbirds can fly a few miles, young men are ready for snacks along the way between planned stops.

No problem, that is, for the car of President Frank L. Peterson who, more laid back and relaxed when he deemed it appropriate, steers his vehicle up to the nearest convenience store for refreshing goodies like crackers, bananas, and cookies. The other car chaperoned by Rabbi Moseley, however, is steered by a spirit of determination to reach their destination and the virtue of holding on for the next 75 to 100 miles or so. Other than the obviously awkward contrast of one car buying while the other car is idling in the park lot, the Peterson crew of students saunter out of the store smiling, even snickering, and holding up their goodies in full view to tempt and tantalize the motionless Moseley group. One can imagine student riders in the Rabbi's car singing many versions of the song: "Milk and honey in-a-dat land one of these days."

The Lost and Last Word

It's a tradition that during the Friday evening Ministerial Seminar (aka Evangeleers or Forum), students from Elder Moseley's homiletics class deliver their sermons to reflect what they had learned about preaching. The audience includes the teacher, class members, and others attending the weekly gathering. Students of the late 1940's or early 1950's would probably remember a certain minister in training giving his sermon using the manuscript method of delivery. Nearing the conclusion of his message, the student preacher looks down and around, shuffling through his pages, and patting his hands against his pants and coat pockets with a quizzical expression on his face. Then he disorientedly says: "I-I don't know what happened. I just don't know. Well, that's all I have to say, brothers and sisters. Now let us *bow our eyes and kneel our heads* in prayer." (Imagine the unbridled laughter) In closing, Elder Moseley prayed: "Oh, Lord, please have mercy on us if you can, if you can."

Unappealing the Appeal

Elder Moseley is distinctly and widely known not only for his teaching but also for church revivals. Just recently, a half century later, Barry Black, Chaplain of the U. S. Senate, was sharing with me how he heard Elder Moseley preaching during a revival in North Carolina where the chaplain was then pastoring. The worship service exalted Jesus Christ and proved so movingly passionate, deeply convicting, and appealingly persuasive until the people literally did not want to go home and in some sense were afraid to dismiss. Heaven was brought so near.

Well, take a visit to the Oakwood campus, Moran Hall auditorium, where the Rabbi is preaching one of his customarily moving sermons for the Communion service. His sermon appeal goes something like this: "Some of you have been in the church for years, and you're *not* converted. Some of you have *never* been converted. I'm inviting all of you who are *not* converted or *never been* converted to *stand*." Several persons take to their feet. Among these respondents is Mrs. Moseley. Apparently not prepared for his own wife of nearly twenty years to respond to such a disclosing appeal, he is reported to have quickly shifted gears with: "Ah, sit down, sit down. You all don't know what I'm talking about." (On the one hand, not many can resist a typically moving Moseley appeal, not even his own household. On the other hand, quick thinking)

Share and Share Alike

A concert tour by the Male Chorus of Oakwood College travels southward to Greenville, Mississippi. Hungry singers are worthy of their hire and are treated to breakfast in a restaurant. Standard procedure is to pass the platter of each food dish around for each person to serve himself and then pass it on until it reaches everybody. But the students are in a playful mood and want to have a little fun. In fact, they're plotting a little trick on the Rabbi. They calculate how much food to take for themselves before the platter reaches their director, Elder Moseley, with little or no food left. The plan works. When the once full platter of food, now nearly empty, gets to the Rabbi, he holds up his plate containing only a thimble of food on it and says with serious and full authority: "All right, you birds, I'm going to pass my plate around and every one of you had better put some of your food back on it." (All in fun, all in stitches, all enjoy a good breakfast.)

To Be or Not to Be

This time the Oakwood student singers are going to Chicago, Illinois. Everybody seems anxious to make the trip but Rabbi Moseley. He's visibly morose and somber and a bit disconcerted. The word leaks out that the Shiloh SDA Church in the windy city is losing its pastor and wants Moseley to fill the vacancy. Somehow, accompanying the singers to an environment seeking his fulltime ministry is not settling well with him. His inner uneasiness wears itself on his countenance and body language. In fact, he's beginning to claim being actually sick to the extent of not attending his Male Chorus concert and appointing a substitute director. President Peterson and others pray for him and then ask: "Elder, what's wrong with you? What is your sickness?" Moseley responds: "I don't know, but I know I'm sick." (His comrades smile to each other, diagnosing that it may not be what it appears.)

To Each His Own

Today is scheduled for classroom preaching. A certain well-known student comes to the homiletics class and presents his sermon. He completes the mechanical letter of the law except, tragic of all tragedies, teacher Moseley recognizes the sermon as essentially and definitely one already delivered by another student. Whether the charge is plagiarism or dishonesty or whatever, the Rabbi assigned the embarrassed student to fulfill the assignment by preparing a sermon on the topic: "The Ministry of Evil Angels." And yes, he had to preach also this second sermon before his classmates.

Congrats or Confession

Many Sabbaths we would ride to church together, Elder and Mrs. Moseley, my fiance' (Barbara, their daughter) and I, and whoever else could fit into the car. He's a member of the General Conference of SDA and living in Takoma Park, Maryland. I'm a student at the SDA Seminary of Potomac University (aka, Andrews University). Elder Moseley is preaching a sermon at the DuPont Park SDA Church in D. C. How well I remember those very first words out of his mouth declaring his sermon's pungent thematic statement: "Conversion is a change." I'm taking notes, resonating very well with his crystal clear Bible support for an important step to a personal relation with Jesus Christ. His use of chalk and black board provided helpful visual making the sermon not only didactic but dynamic and direct. I am touched both as a worshipper and as a major in homiletics at the seminary. When the service is over and we all pack into the car, I express my appreciation to the Rabbi: "Very informative and persuasive message, Elder. I was helped very much." His curious response: "O-oh, you were '*helped*' "? I know not how to express here his tone of voice on paper, but his emphasis on the word "helped" suggested to me that my intended *compliment* is being interpreted to be a *confession.* If so, on hindsight, it was risky to inadvertently give my fiance's father the impression that I am struggling with some mortal transgression and thereby unsuitable to marry his daughter. (But apparently no harm done. Barb and I married on schedule with his full blessings. Amen.)

Can You Top This?

Occasionally, when a seminary student in Takoma Park, Maryland, I would visit the General Conference offices of Elders Frank Loris Peterson, E. Earl Cleveland, and Calvin Edwin Moseley. The two buildings are just across the walkway from each other.

I'm anxious to unload on them some newfangled theological nugget from class which I find exciting and worth telling somebody else about it. So up the stairs I skip first to the office of Elder Cleveland who unfailingly inflates my ego with something like: "Wow! Man, that's great stuff! Let me get my notebook to write that down. Keep it coming. Keep on feeding my mind and filling my files." From there, I go to Elder Peterson's office. While I'm unloading on him my freshly learned seminary theology, he waits patiently for me to get through it all then says to me almost sympathetically but with a smile: "Young man, keep it to yourself." Next I enter the office of Elder Moseley, incidentally my father-in-law to be, who also gives me a hearing with hand on his chin, eyes locked on me closely, and a smile. I run my latest seminary knowledge by him, and right on queue as it were, he counters with some theological gem he considers as good or better than mine. He does it all in good spirit, fair repartee, and a smile that says "top that if you can." (I do wonder if he's trying to remind me that he attended and graduated with an M. A. degree from the same seminary or maybe I'm a mere "Johnny-come-lately." Is this a forecast of intellectual sparring awaiting us around the family dinner table over years to come?)

Saturday Night Wise

Two Oakwood coeds are exiting the Moran Hall auditorium on a Saturday night. A lovely evening together at the lyceum concert! Perhaps better than the musical itself were those tender moments of social interaction. At such times, concerts can never be any too long. Nevertheless, you never know what curious eyes or color commentary might be near. And so it was. The female student on this date happens to be daughter of the Oakwood president. The young man, one of Moseley's aspiring ministers in training. The Rabbi captures the moment with an added dimension of what it means to really "aspire" when he's heard to remark: "Boy, he shonuff knows where to hang his hat."

Take 6, 7, 8 or?

That the Moseley gene encoded his unique music ability for himself and his offspring is quite evident. He practically taught himself to blow the cornet and trumpet and sang in choral groups when a student at Tuskegee Institute and Oakwood Junior College during the 1920's and directed such groups when he became an Oakwood teacher. Before Oakwood, he played in school bands at Jackson State College and Tuskegee Institute and then at Oakwood Junior College. When a student and teacher at Oakwood, he regularly blew his cornet/trumpet for congregational singing, special programs, and personal enjoyment. His developing skill and artistry with the instrument improved continually. Whether he took additional instruction at Oakwood is not known. He does mention in his archival papers that he highly regarded and appreciated listening to an extraordinary trumpeter named "Mr. (James) Wilson" of Alabama A&M University from across town in Huntsville. Occasionally, Wilson performed for the Oakwood campus accompanied on the piano by Dr. Henry Bradford who himself, as A&M University chaplain, became a favorite chapel speaker at Oakwood (his wife, Nell Bradford, directing the famous A&M choir). I personally recall hearing Wilson's beautiful trumpeting in his senior years during my early Oakwood student days beyond the years of Moseley. Philosophically, I came to understand that a musical instrument (whether trumpet or drum or piano, etc.) comes to a person as ethically neutral in itself, without being good or bad, acceptable or unacceptable. Talent awaits usage by the possessor to determine right or wrong, appropriate or inappropriate. As an immediate graduate of Oakwood Junior College, 1927, Calvin Moseley, Jr. was invited to render special music for the General Conference of SDA in Milwaukee, Wisconsin. He played a classical piece on his trumpet entitled "The Commodore Polka" by W. Paris Chambers which requires dexterity and grace for the triple tonguing expertise.

Fast forward to the 1950's when his two daughters both revealed special talent for music in academy and college succeeded by their own children (Moseley's grandchildren and great grandchildren).

Residing in the Oakwood University community during his retirement, particularly the 1980's, Moseley was privileged to see one of his grands, Merv, come to be known on campus and later nationally and internationally as an extraordinarily gifted musician ("Take 6," et cetera) not just natively so but educationally as well (B.A. in music from Oakwood University and M.A. in music composition and arrangement from University of Alabama). I think my point is this. A dear friend of mine and former student of Elder Moseley telephoned me and shared similar thoughts expressed above. That is to say, the same rare ear and mind for music, the ingenuous arrangement, hearing things from the spheres as it were or from the tenth muse, which the rest of us do not hear musically, that rare genius broke through in the music of "Mose" as in the music of grandson "Merv." A member of student choral groups by Moseley in his musical prime, Calvin Rock recollects: "When we sang in the Male Chorus directed by Elder Moseley, until he patiently revealed it to us, we as singers could not *hear* what he was hearing or *perceive* of those intricate musical chords he was conceptualizing."

So I got to thinking. *What if* there had been no wide sixty-year generation gulf separating Elder Moseley the college student of the 1920's and his grandson, Mervyn, the college student of the 1980's? *What if* there had been no serious religio-cultural clashes between musical styles, genres, and sensitivities surrounding the appropriate and inappropriate? *What if* the generation *gulf* had shrunk at least no more than to a *gap* toward a closer merger when Elder Moseley's granddaughter, Karmen Keith, honored him with her keyboard solo rendition of the spiritual "Give Me Jesus" in contemporary style at his memorial celebration February 5, 2001? *What if* the Moseley genes, perpetuated through his parade of progeny, would have *collaborated* at some point in their common lifetimes to write, arrange, perform, and produce a piece of music *together*—a composition for the ages! What a team they would have been! For some of us, it may sound incredulous! For others, it's incredible! Or, it may just be something else to smile about.

AND SO ON

We conclude our lighthearted moments from the days of the Rabbi but not from lack of more examples. The quiver has many more. One more brief example will take you back to Moseley giving encouraging evaluation of sermons delivered by budding preachers in his homiletics class. Sometime when a student fell short of the expected mark, the Rabbi might say along the way: *"Your peach ain't ripe"* or he might advise: *"Little ships should stay close to the shore."* One homiletics student is very late with the perennial assignment of writing the sermon outline on the board *before* class gets started so that fellow students can follow during his presentation. This particular student missed his "before class" deadline and is taking the lion's share of the regular class period trying hurriedly to write his sermon on the board. As the atmosphere thickens with tenseness, students wait and watch nervously for the student's sake. By this time, Rabbi Moseley takes his characteristic pose of hanging his forehead in hand when sorely displeased. At long last, the student is still not finished writing but feeling constrained to break the silence he says: "Elder Moseley, I'm not finished yet." To which the teacher responds: *"Today, you were finished from the very beginning."* (The class couldn't restrain itself in laughter. And the Rabbi? Even he could not miss the spontaneous humor of the moment)

Well, these are a few of many lighthearted mementos from those who loved the Rabbi. Perhaps somebody someday will preserve a collection of like gems to relax our overly tense moments. Remember: "A merry heart is good medicine." (Proverbs 17:22, NIV)

OAKWOOD UNIVERISTY CHURCH PASTORS SUCCESIVE TO CALVIN E. MOSELEY, JR., ITS FIRST AFRICAN AMERICAN PASTOR

Calvin Edwin Moseley, Jr. (1934-1951)

Robert L. Woodfork (1951-1953)

Clarence T. Richards (1953-1955)

Jessie R. Wagner (1955-1956)

Joseph T. Stafford (1956-1959)

John J. Beale (1959-1961)

Ned Lindsay (c. 1961-?)

Richard E. Tottress (1969-1971)

William L. DeShay (1971-1972)

Eric C. Ward (1973-1994)

Leslie N. Pollard (1994-1997)

John S. Nixon (1997-2006)

Craig Newborn (2006-2011)

Carlton P. Byrd (2012-present)

Sources

1. *Adventist Review*, "Father of Preachers," August, 2000 (Adaptation of Ben Johnson's original article by same title in *Huntsville Times*, January 30, 2000)
2. A variety of notes, records, memorabilia, *Spreading Oaks (Student Paper)*, etc., in the Archives of the Eva B. Dykes Library of Oakwood University, Huntsville, AL.
3. Dykes, James. " 'Called to Preach' (A Pen Portrait of Calvin Edwin Moseley, Jr.)", Undated/c. 1980's, Unpublished, a brief biographical essay by the former Editor of the *Message Magazine*, Archives of the Eva B. Dykes Library of Oakwood University, Huntsville, AL.
4. Fordham, Walter W. *Righteous Rebel (The Unforgettable Legacy of a Fearless Advocate for Change),* Washington, D. C.: Review and Publishing Association, 1990.
5. Johnson, Ben. "The Father of Preachers," *The Huntsville Times*, January 30, 2000 (All other articles by this title are adapted from this *original* feature)
6. Kelly, Andria and Dawn Miles. "The Father of Preachers," *Southern Tidings*, March, 2001 (These two interns of Oakwood U. Public Relations adapted this article from the original by Ben Johnson of the *Huntsville Times*, January 30, 2000)
7. Moseley, Calvin E., Jr. "Providences" (A handwritten essay by Moseley himself about thirty pages in length giving an autobiographical overview of key focal points in his life/Undated), Archives of the Eva B. Dykes Library, Oakwood University.
8. *Oakwood College Magazine*, "The Father of Preachers," Spring, 2001 (Adaptation of Ben Johnson's original article

by the same title in *Huntsville Times*, January 30, 2000)

9. Reynolds, Louis B. *We Have Tomorrow (The Story of American Seventh-day Adventists with an African Heritage),* Washington, D.C.: Review and Herald Publishing Association, 1984.

10. Rock, Clara (Peterson), Archivist of Eva B. Dykes Library. A vis-à-vis interview of Elder Calvin E. Moseley, Jr., 1974, just after his retirement from the General Conference of Seventh-day Adventists.

11. Rodger, Emanuel, "The Life and Contributions of Calvin Edwin Moseley, Jr.," a research paper for Sociology of Religion class at Oakwood University, presented to Dr. Calvin B. Rock, teacher, Winter Quarter, 1974. (Dr. Rock was also president of the institution at the time); Archives of the Eva B. Dykes Library of Oakwood University.

12. Starks, Walter M., "The Beloved Rabbi: Biography of Elder C. E. Moseley, Jr.," 1988, Unpublished, an eighty-eight page document of Elder Moseley by one who had been his former student at Oakwood Junior College during the early 1940's, a successful pastor, conference president, and stewardship leader in the General Conference of SDA.

13. Warren, Mervyn A. *Oakwood! A Vision Splendid Continues (1896-2010),* the centennial history of Oakwood University, Collegedale: College Press, 2010.

14. Finally, the most proximate source of all—Barbara Jean (Moseley) Warren, the younger daughter of Elder Calvin E. Moseley, Jr. and my endearing wife.

Index

Abernathy, Ralph D., 86
Advanced Bible School, 78
Alabama A&M University, 90
Allison, Jonathan, 77
Allison, Thomas, 60–62
Anderson, Alan, Jr., 77
Anderson, R. Allan, 86, 87
Arms, J. K., 41, 47
"Aunt Ethel" (Moseley), 77
Aunt Minnie, 13, 14, 17, 23

Bailey, Alga, 37
Baker, Delbert W., 87
Baker, Trevor, 74
Baker, W. L. H., 30, 53
Banfield, Warren, 87
Banks, Rosa, 87
Barron, Richard, 87
Bates, Russell, 87
Battle, Maurice (Esther), 87, 91
Baugh, Julia, 37, 66
Beardsley, J. I., 33
Berean Church (St. Louis, MO), 64
Black, Barry, 108
Bland, Louis, 73
Blanchard, Irene, 63
Blanks, Marie, 63
Blevins, Marian, 63
Blue, Dedrick, 99
Bradford, Charles E., 73, 87, 89
Bradford-Cleveland-Brooks Leadership Center, 73
Bradford, Henry, 113
Bradford, Nell, 113
Branson, W. H., 81–83, 85–87
Brooks, Charles D., 73, 87
Brown, Ruby, 63
Browne, Benjamin, 74
Bryant, Alex, 74, 87
Byers, Ashlee, 89
Byers, Asia, 89
Byers, Autumn, 89
Byers, Ayana, 89

Byers, Timothy, 89
Byers, Shana (Warren), 89
Byrd, Carlton, 99

Cantrell, Paul, 104
Careful Builders Club, 23
Carter, Robert H., 63
Carver, George Washington, 19–22, 24, 25, 29
Cheatham, Charles, 78
Christian, Ivan, 33
Christian, J. W., 84
Christian, L. H., 50
Christian, Percy, 54
Cleveland, E. Earl, 73, 85–87
Clinton Theological Seminary, 36
Columbia Union College, 71, 78, 81, 88
Crowe, Daniel W., 63
Cunningham, Charles, 75
Cunningham, Eugenia, 74, 75

Daniel, Lucius (Naomi), 91
Dascent, J. G., 73
Davis, Jerome, 74
Demopolis, AL, 9–11, 15, 22, 27, 41
Dent, Joseph F., 63
Dillett, Eric, 63
Dixon, Lillie Belle, 9–11, 27, 39, 51, 63
Dixon, James Hughes, 10, 40
Dobson, Imani, 95
Dobson, Michael, Jr., 89
Dykes, Eva B., 68

Edgecombe, James, A., 73, 86
Edwards, Otis, B., 38
Eggleston, Lilage, 79
Emmanuel Missionary College (aka Andrews University), 31, 36, 37, 39–42, 49, 51, 54, 57, 58, 62, 65, 66, 78

Figuhr, R. R., 87
First SDA Church (Huntsville, AL), 79
Fisk Jubilee Singers, 34

Flood, James, 23
Fordham, Walter W., Sr., 73, 77
Frazier, Ruth, 63
Fullard, Lamar, 90
Fullard, Larry, 90
Fullard, Larry, Jr., 90
Fullard, Lori (Keith), 90

General Conference Session of 1927, 38, 39
Giddings, Phillip (Violet), 91
Gray, Charles, 38
Graysville, TN, 37
Great Depression, 49, 59
Green, Herbert, 54, 55, 69
Green, W. H., 84

Hale, Frank, II, 64
Hall, Harriet Slater, 63
Hammond, Henry, 34
Haysmer, A. J., 84
Hemsley, Rose, 63
Henri, Dunbar (Lorraine), 91
Hinsdale Hospital, 37, 58, 66, 71
Howard, T. R. M., 71
Howard University, 19, 68, 78
Howard U. Divinity School, 78
Huddleston, S. B., 38
Humphrey, J. K., 38, 52, 53

Illinois Conference, 47, 49
Imes, G. Lake, 23

Jackson, Daniel R., 88
Jackson State College, 28, 33, 34, 65, 68, 113
Jacobsen, E. E., 36
Jarreau, Emile, 38, 50, 53, 63
Joiner, Murray, 87
Jones, Alfred, 29
Jones, Ed, 11
Jones, Frank, 87
Jones, Principal, 18
Jones, Mrs. T. Ann, 36

Keith, Dennis, 87
Keith, Donald, 90
Keith, Harriet Ann (Moseley), 90
Keith, Karmen, 90, 114
Keitts, Frederick S., 27, 28

Kibble, Harvey, Sr., 38
Kimbrough, Mr/Mrs A. W., 79
King, Martin Luther, Jr., 86, 92
Knight, Anna, 33

Lake Region Conference, 72, 89
Laurence, J. H., 27
Lee, Althea, 88
Lee, Genesee (Jennie), 23, 28
Lee, Harold, 73
Lewis, James, 74
Lockett, Edgar, 96

Madison School, 36
Mendinghall, V. J., 74
Message Magazine, 67
"Miss Slater," 36, 39, 57
Missouri Conference, 60
Mitchell, Leland (Lottie), 91
Monk, Camela (Crawford), 103
Monk, Paul, 103
Moran, James L., 64, 65, 68, 79, 81, 82, 84
Moseley, Augusta, 90
Moseley, Barbara Jean, 74, 93
Moseley, Calvin E., Sr., 9–12, 17, 27, 33, 39, 51
Moseley, Eddie, 90
Moseley, Ernest, Jr., 90
Moseley, Ernest, Sr., 10–12, 17, 27, 33, 38, 40, 76, 77, 90
Moseley, Ethel, 90
Moseley, Harriet Ann, 66, 71, 90
Moseley, Harriet Frances (Slater), 70, 71, 90, 91
Moseley, Lillie Belle (Dixon), 9–11, 27, 39, 51, 63
Moton, Robert, 20, 23
Murphy, George, 63
Murphy, Herman, 73, 77
Myers, Samuel, 87

North American Division, 59, 71, 82, 83, 86, 88, 93
Northwestern University, 36, 54

Oakwood College Alumni Assn., 79
Oakwood College Church, 79
Oakwood Jubilee Quartette, 34
Oakwood Junior College, 35, 38, 40, 63, 64, 68

INDEX

Oakwood University, 88, 89
Ochs, Dan, 36

Partridge, Gaines R., 77
Pearson, Walter, 87
Perkins, Addison, 40
Peters, George E., 50–54, 69, 80, 82–84, 90
Peterson, Frank L., 27, 34, 35, 37, 38, 83–85, 87, 97, 107, 110–112
Phipps, Wintley, 87
Pine Forge Academy, 89
Pollard, Leslie N., 84

Rashford, Samuel, 77
Reaves, Benjamin F., 86
Regional Conferences, 72, 73, 87, 95
Regional Conference Presidents (first ones), 73
Regional Conference Presidents (year 2005), 74
Reynolds, Louis B., 70, 98
Richards, Clarence T., 68
Riverside Hospital, 71
Rock, Calvin B., 73, 87, 97, 98, 114
Rock, Clara (Peterson), 46, 66, 78
Rogers, Ernest, 68
Rowe, T. M., 73

Salisberry, Charles, 34
Saulter, H. T., 63
Scales, William, 86
SDA Seminary, 78
Shelton, Lillie Belle (Moseley), 90
Shepperd, Elbert W., 86
Shiloh Church (Chicago), 37, 54, 55, 62, 63
Shuler, J. L., 78
Singleton, Harold, 73
Slater, Fred, 63
Slater, Harriet Frances, 37, 57–59, 63
South Atlantic Conference, 74, 85
Southern Adventist Univeristy (Graysville, TN), 37

Southern Union, 85
Soyasen, Cris P., 54
Starks, Walter, 73, 87
Stephenson, C. B., 84
Stratton, Jennie, 37
Student Strike (1932), 76

"Take 6," 114
Taylor, Viola, 37
Taylor, Willie, 74
Thomas, Phenicie Skinner, 46
Thompson, W. A., 73
Thurman, Howard, 78
Troy, Owen, Sr., 62, 63, 65
Troy, Ruby, 63
Tucker, Joseph A., 31, 33–35, 39

Vandeman, George, 71
Van Putten, Meade, 87
Vaughn, Rose Marie, 63
Verdun, Lovey (Davis), 63

Wagner, John H., Sr., 34, 37–38
Ward, Eric C., 96, 99
Warren, Barbara J. (Moseley), 89
Warren, Eugene, 89
Warren, Karis, 89
Warren, Malachiae, 89
Warren, Mervyn Edwin, 89, 114
Warren, Shana, 89
Warren, Shelli, 89
Washington, Booker T., 19, 20
Washington, Frances (Moseley), 90
Webb, William, 68
Weiss-Sledge Family Reunion, 11
White, Ellen G., 30, 31, 35, 71
Williams, DeWitt, 87
Wilson, James (A&M U.), 113
Wilson, Ted N. C., 88
Wolfkill, Guy F., 41–43
Woodfork, Robert L., 87
Wright, Billy, 74
Wright, Henry, 88

About the Author

Mervyn A. Warren is a son-in-law of Elder Calvin Edwin Moseley, Jr. He had the privilege of following Moseley (decades later) in the self-same position (Dean of Religion) where Moseley himself served for seventeen years (1934-1951). Warren graduated from Oakwood University (B.A.), SDA Seminary of Andrews University (M.A., M.Div.), Michigan State University (Ph.D.), and Vanderbilt Divinity School (D.Min.). He has held more major leadership positions at Oakwood University than anyone else in the history of the institution:

Dean of the School of Religion, General Vice President (combining Academic Affairs and Student Services), Vice President for Academic Affairs, Assistant to the President, Provost and Senior Vice President, and Interim President. In addition to a host of professional articles, he authored "Knowing That We Know God," (Adult Sabbath School Lessons for spring, 1984) and the following books: 1) *God Made Known*; 2) *Ellen G. White on Preaching*; 3) *Black Preaching: Truth and Soul*; 4) *King Came Preaching (Pulpit Power of Martin Luther King, Jr.)*; 5) *Sprucing the Tree/Up Close from the Inside (Saga of Oakwood University Presidents, 1896-2015*; 6) *Oakwood! A Vision Splendid Continues (1896-2010)*, the latter being the official centennial history of that university. He is married to the younger daughter of Elder Moseley, Barbara Jean, and their family includes: sons Eugene and Mervyn Edwin and daughters Karis Warren and Shana Warren-Byers and eight grandchildren: Ashlee, Asia, Autumn, Ayana, Imani, Malachiae, Michael, Jr. and Shelli.